Modern
PRIVATE OWNL..
WAGONS
on British Rail

Modern
PRIVATE OWNER
WAGONS
on British Rail

David Ratcliffe

Patrick Stephens Limited

First published in 1989

British Library Cataloguing in Publication Data

Ratcliffe, David
  Modern private owner wagons on British Rail
  1. Great Britain. Railway services.
  British Rail. Privately owned goods wagons
  I. Title
  625.2'4'0941

  ISBN 1-85260-062-4

Front cover illustrations (Clockwise, from top left) CAWD 92717, a 41 ton two-axle container wagon loaded with a purpose-built coal container (*A. Prime*); a liquid chlorine tank leased to ICI Mond by Tiger Rail; one of a small fleet of 88 ton hoppers owned by Hall Aggregates to carry sea-dredged gravel (*A. Prime*); a 90 ton aggregate hopper used to carry 'hardstone' from Bardon Hill Quarry.

Patrick Stephens Limited is part of the Thorsons Publishing Group, Wellingborough, Northamptonshire, NN8 2RQ, England.

Printed by Woolnough Bookbinding Limited, Irthlingborough, Northamptonshire

10 9 8 7 6 5 4 3 2 1

Contents

Preface			6
Chapter	1	Introduction: The Fall and Rise of the Private Owner Wagon	7
Chapter	2	Covered Hopper Wagons	13
Chapter	3	Bulk Powder Wagons	25
Chapter	4	Flat Wagons	37
Chapter	5	Open Hopper Wagons	51
Chapter	6	Motor Vehicle Carrying Wagons	65
Chapter	7	Mineral Wagons, Opens and Tipplers	71
Chapter	8	Vans and Coaches	91
Chapter	9	Miscellaneous and Special Wagons	99
Chapter	10	Tank Wagons of below 40 tonnes glw	113
Chapter	11	Tank Wagons of 40 tonnes to 51 tonnes glw	126
Chapter	12	Bogie Tank Wagons	151
Index			167

Preface

This book presents a pictorial survey of one of the most colourful and interesting aspects of the modern railway scene, the private owner wagon, and covers all the British privately-owned stock, including British-registered ferry vehicles, that has operated on British Rail since 1976. Except where an obvious anomaly exists, such as in the classification of many bogie open wagons, the broad wagon categories used by TOPS have been adopted, with each category being discussed chapter by chapter.

Within the tables, all wagons are listed in order of type along with their TOPS code and build details, together with their original owners and operators, where the latter differed from the former. Usually a complete block of numbers is used by an owner/operator for a particular type of wagon, but in those cases where gaps exist within a number series this is indicated by (r); ie vehicles are numbered within the number range quoted. For clarity, the 12th digit, referred to as the computer check digit, has been omitted from the numbers of *RIV* vehicles, hence the listing of 11-digit rather than 12-digit numbers. All references to weight are shown in metric tonnes and the abbreviation 'glw' is used to express gross laden weight.

Many people have helped during the preparation of this book and I should like to acknowledge the generous assistance given by L. Brunton from the Tyne & Wear Passenger Transport Executive, J. Morton of John Walker & Sons Limited, D. Tandy from The Standard Railway Wagon Company, M. Vanstone of Cumbria Engineering, and fellow enthusiasts D. Monk-Steel and R. Wallace. Special thanks go to P. Bartlett, A. Dasi-Sutton, P. Fidczuk, D. Larkin, T. Mann, A. Prime, D. Rowland, and R. Silsbury for permission to use a number of their photographs. However, all opinions, errors and omissions are my own.

David Ratcliffe

Chapter 1

Introduction: The Fall and Rise of the Private Owner Wagon

The era of the private owner wagon appeared to have all but drawn to a close following the nationalization of Britain's railways in 1948. All such vehicles that were capable of general use had been taken over by the Ministry of War Transport at the outbreak of war in 1939, and those that survived the rigours of wartime then passed directly into British Railways' ownership to eke out their few remaining years in common use. The only wagons to avoid both wartime pooling and subsequent nationalization were a few specialist types such as tipplers, which required special unloading facilities, and tanks, which carried specialized commodities. Most fleets were composed largely of elderly vehicles, often built before the Grouping of 1923, and rapidly approaching the end of their useful lives.

The early 1950s witnessed a further decline with few privately-owned wagons being built, for although British Railways was actively developing a number of new and innovative wagon types itself, its policy was to discourage private ownership of all but tank wagons. However, during the second half of the decade a significant advance in wagon design, coinciding with an easing of attitudes towards the building of privately-owned wagons intended for block–train operation, marked the beginnings of a remarkable resurgence in the fortunes of the private owner wagon.

In 1957 a new 35 t tank design appeared, developed as a result of collaboration between British Railways, Esso Petroleum and wagon builders Charles Roberts. The tank had a slightly improved capacity over earlier vehicles but, more importantly, was fitted with roller bearing axle-boxes and automatic vacuum brakes, which, when combined with the 15 ft wheel-base, enabled high-speed operation. The design was an immediate success and quickly went into quantity production for Esso and a number of other petroleum and chemical companies (see Chapter 10). Further technical advance followed in the shape of the 'monobloc' tank (see Chapter 11) which allowed for the construction of wagons with increased tank diameters and substantially improved payloads. By 1964, a 46 t monobloc design had become the new standard and remained in production until the end of the decade as all the major oil companies invested heavily in new tank wagons and loading facilities, while gradually building up a rail-served network of oil-handling terminals throughout the country.

From 1966, the maximum permitted axle-load was increased from $22\frac{1}{2}$ t to 25 t, while the more efficient air brake replaced the traditional vacuum brake on all new construction. The improved economics of rail transport, made possible by larger wagons and faster transits, now encouraged other companies, particularly in the cement industry, to invest in their own fleet of wagons, and as the insistence on block-train working was relaxed, more new types were introduced. By the early 1970s, British Rail's policy had come full circle — from then on, it would only provide wagons for general merchandise traffic and for the nationalized industries and government departments, while other customers were to be encouraged to provide their own wagons, both for new traffics and to replace life-expired railway-owned wagons in existing traffics as the latter were withdrawn from service.

This policy, with one notable exception, remains largely unchanged to the present day, and the intervening years have seen a steadily increasing number of privately-owned wagons take to the rails, carrying a wide variety of traffics including such diverse items as furniture, petfood and domestic refuse. Continuous improvements in wagon design have furthered this process, while the financial policy of successive governments has also encouraged companies to either invest in their own wagon fleet, or else hire, or more likely lease, wagons from one of the major hirers such as Procor, Railease, or Tiger Railcar Leasing. Apart from the smaller initial financial outlay involved in leasing, a major advantage is that the hire companies make all the arrangements for the maintenance of their wagons. Since 1974, direct Government support in the form of grant aid, known as a 'Section 8 Grant', has been available to defray up to 60 per cent of the cost of new rail-freight installations and wagons in those cases where the use of rail transport would result in significant benefits to the environment.

Furthermore, by 1984 British Rail had

The success of the Speedlink network has played a major part in the advance of the private owner wagon. Here 47 233 hauls the 08.56 Eastleigh to Severn Tunnel Junction, one of the few daytime services, past Dean Hill on 24 February 1986 when composed entirely of private owner stock, including an empty MoD 'Warwell', five STS slurry tanks, three APCM cement Presflos, and a handful of petroleum tanks (A. Dasi-Sutton).

completely replaced its old-fashioned wagon-load freight system, which had suffered from problems of low speed, frequent re-marshalling and unreliable service, with a modern high-speed air-braked network known as 'Speedlink'. The Speedlink network is based upon a number of carefully controlled, exclusively air-braked overnight trunk services linking a dozen or so main yards where they exchange traffic. However, there is no marshalling in the traditional sense *en route*, trains stopping only to exchange pre-formed sections, so that a wagon is only shunted twice, once in its originating area and again at its destination.

Such has been the success of this service that many customers, particularly in the lucrative distribution business, who only a few years ago would have looked askance at the idea of using rail, now consider Railfreight an attractive proposition — indeed, there are wagon operators who find it worthwhile to place a single vehicle on to rail.

Another development of considerable benefit to the private wagon operator has been the adoption by British Rail of a real-time computer system to regulate its entire operation. Developed from a system pioneered by the Southern Pacific Railroad in the USA, it was gradually introduced on British Rail from 1971, the whole country being finally covered by 1975. Always known by its acronym TOPS, the Total Operations Processing System records each event affecting vehicles as it happens, allowing for the constant monitoring of a wagon's movements and availability, which, when taken in conjunction with the fast turn rounds made possible by Speedlink, leads to much greater utilization of a company's fleet.

In order to provide information in a straightforward and uniform manner compatible with the needs of a computerized system of control, a new set of wagon codes had to be devised to replace the rather antiquated telegraphic codes formerly in use. The new TOPS codes are based on a four-letter code in which each letter conveys information, and which, when taken together, provide a detailed description of the vehicle. The first letter defines the broad

Modern freight wagons carry an information panel showing the vehicle's tare weight, capacity and TOPS code, as well as the individual wagon number. This example belongs to the prototype 'In-line tippler', REDA 28100, built by Standard Wagon in 1987.

grouping of wagon type to which the individual vehicle belongs (privately-owned wagons occupy both the 'P' and 'T' groups) while the second letter defines more exactly the wagon type in question (see Tables 1 and 2). The third letter of the code indicates the brake type of the wagon, referring to the fitting of through pipes where appropriate, as well as to the provision of full automatic brakes (see Table 3). The fourth letter refers to sub-divisions within each type.

To assist operating staff, the first three letters of this code are included on a wagon's information panel, normally to be found painted on the side of the vehicle. The panel also carries details as to the wagon's tare weight, expressed in kilo-grams, and its capacity, shown in tonnes. The bottom line carries the wagon's TOPS number consisting of a four- or five-digit number (ie a figure between 1000 and 99999), prefixed by an abbreviated form of the owner's name, consisting of up to four letters.

Before the introduction of TOPS, each wagon owner decided upon his own numbering policy with the result that some numbers, particularly those below 100, were repeated over and over again. Existing wagons were therefore renumbered into the new system prior to 1975, and all new wagons have been allocated TOPS numbers as they have been registered to run on British Rail. As ferry-fitted vehicles

Privately-owned wagons operate to all corners of the railway network. On 26 August 1987, 47 144 nears Aller Junction with a St Blazey to Severn Tunnel Junction service, which inludes one of the Cadoux-built, Tiger Rail covered hoppers used in calcified seaweed traffic (the third wagon in the train), two 'Tullis Russell' china clay covered hoppers, and a selection of tank wagons including Class A, LPG, and bitumen (A. Dasi-Sutton).

already carried computerized numbers in the UIC 12-digit system, they required no change. To ensure the integrity of the system, each number is now unique to the wagon carrying it, there being no cases of numbers being either duplicated or re-used. The only alterations occur in the case of major rebuilding, when a fresh number is allocated, or in cases of a change of owner-ship, which are reflected in a change of prefix. Furthermore, a number of wagons acquired by Shell and by British Petroleum have been subsequently renumbered so as to conform with the number coding used by both companies.

In 1975, privately-owned wagons repres-ented some 13 per cent of the total freight fleet by number, while their contents were approaching 28 per cent of British Rail's freight tonnage. Since then, the construc-tion of numerous fleets of modern wagons capable of carrying increased payloads, together with the upgrading of many older vehicles, has seen these figures rise dramatically. At the time of writing, privately-owned wagons account for nearly 32 per cent of the total wagon stock and carry almost 50 per cent of all rail-hauled freight. The resurgence of the private owner wagon is all but complete, as they can now be found operating from almost every corner of the rail network, carrying virtually all types of railborne traffic.

Table 1: *TOPS code group 'P' — all privately-owned wagons other than tanks*

TOPS code	Description
PA	Covered hopper wagon, two-axle
PB	Covered hopper wagon, bogie
PC	Bulk powder wagon, compressed air discharge, two-axle
PD	Bulk powder wagon, compressed air discharge, bogie
PE	Tip-Air bulk powder wagon, two-axle
PF	Flat wagon
PG	Hopper wagon, two-axle
PH	Hopper wagon, bogie
PI	International ferry wagon *RIV*, British registered
PJ	Cartic, articulated two-tier car carrier set, bogie
PK	Comtic, articulated commercial vehicle carrier set, three-axle
PL	Two-tier car carrier wagon, bogie
PM	Mineral wagon, two-axle
PN	Open pallet wagon, bogie
PO	Open wagon, two-axle
PP	Escort coach/weedkilling train coach, bogie
PQ	Autic, articulated two-tier car carrier set, three-axle
PR	Mineral wagon, curtain-roof, two-axle
PS	Tippler wagon, two-axle
PT	Tippler wagon, bogie
PV	Van/Palvan, two-axle
PW	Van/Palvan, bogie
PX	Miscellaneous or special wagon

Table 2: *TOPS code group 'T' — tanks (British privately-owned)*

TOPS code	Description
TA	Tank wagon, bogie, 40–69 tonnes glw
TB	Tank wagon, bogie, 70–79 tonnes glw
TC	Tank wagon, bogie, 80–89 tonnes glw
TD	Tank wagon, bogie, 90–99 tonnes glw
TE	Tank wagon, bogie, over 100 tonnes glw
TI	Tank wagon, *RIV*, British registered, all types
TM	Tank wagon, three-axle, 25 tonnes glw
TR	Tank wagon, two-axle, 20–29 tonnes glw
TS	Tank wagon, two-axle, 30–39 tonnes glw
TT	Tank wagon, two- or three-axle, 40–49 tonnes glw
TU	Tank wagon, two-axle, over 50 tonnes glw

Table 3: *TOPS brake-type codes*

(Used as suffix to the two-letter codes listed in Tables 1 & 2)

A	Air-braked
B	Air-braked, vacuum through pipe
F	Vacuum (AFI)-braked
G	Vacuum (AFI)-braked, air through pipe
H	Dual-braked, air and vacuum (AFI)
O	Unfitted
P	Vacuum through pipe
Q	Air through pipe
R	Dual air and vacuum through pipes
V	Vacuum-braked
W	Vacuum-braked, air through pipe
X	Dual-braked, air and vacuum

Chapter 2

Covered Hopper Wagons

Covered hopper wagons are designed to carry loads that need protection from the weather and can at the same time be easily discharged by gravity. Following nationalization, British Railways provided the general purpose 'Covhop' wagon, as well as a separate type for grain traffic, but these have been gradually replaced by the growing numbers of privately-owned wagons listed in Tables 4 and 5.

Table 4: *Covered hopper wagons, two-axle*

Type	Number series		TOPS code	Builder	Date	Owner/Operator
Grain	SGD	7906–7948(r)	PAO	Hurst Nelson	1937	Scottish Grain Distillers
Grain	BCH	7801–7824	PAO	Various	1958	Bass Charrington
Grain	BRT	7500–7799	PAF	Various	1965–71	BRTE/various
Grain/Aggregate	PR	14152–14175	PGA	Procor	1975	Procor/various
Lime	PR	8000–8049	PAB	Standard Wagon	1970	Procor/various
Lime	BRT	8050–8118	PAA	Standard Wagon	1972	BRTE/British Steel
Lime	BSGL	8150–8199	PAA	BREL Ashford	1974	British Steel, Glasgow
Lime/Iron ore	BSRV	12500–12599	PGA	Various	1979	British Steel, Ravenscraig
Lime	STET	18700–18729	PAA	Standard Wagon	1981	Steetley Refractories
Alumina	ALCN	12017–12035	PAO	BREL Ashford	1971	Alcan, Lynemouth
Petroleum coke	BRT	12100–12116	PAB	BREL Doncaster	1970	BRTE/Anglesey Aluminium
China clay	TRL	12800–12807	PAA	Standard Wagon	1981	Tiger Rail/Tullis Russell
Sand	BIS	7825–7844	PAA	Standard Wagon	1982	British Industrial Sand
Sand	BIS	7950–7989	PAA	W.H. Davis	1981	British Industrial Sand

Grain hoppers, two-axle

Grain traffic has always been of considerable importance since its seasonal nature, and the long distances often involved in its transportation, make it ideally suitable for rail haulage in bulk. Traditionally, grain has been moved in railway-owned wagons although the Scottish Grain Distillers owned a fleet of unfitted 31 t glw, $20\frac{1}{2}$ t capacity hoppers, built in 1937 to an LMS design, for carrying malt from the Scottish Lowlands to their distilleries in north-east Scotland. In some ways a forerunner of the 'Blues' detailed below, five of this type, SGD 7906/18/26/46/48, survived long enough to receive TOPS numbers and could be found working out of Windygates Distillery, Cameron Bridge, until final withdrawal in 1981. Their attractive livery comprised a grey body and solebar, SGD initials and all other lettering in white-shaded maroon, and black springs and brake gear.

Bass Charrington also owned a fleet of unfitted 31 t glw grain hoppers for carrying malted barley from East Anglia to its breweries in Burton-on-Trent. They were originally railway-owned vehicles, but were transferred to private ownership in 1967, remaining in use until the late 1970s when the traffic went over to road. The first 12 were built to the old LMS all-steel bulk grain design, and remainder to the standard British Railways specification. Both versions could carry 20 t of grain loaded through two sliding roof–hatches with gravity discharge via a single hopper. Shoe suspension was common to all 24 wagons, the original livery being overall grey with a separate 'Bass' nameplate; later, all were repainted red with 'Bass Charrington' lettering in white, painted directly on to the wagon side, and black underframes.

All these early vehicles owed much to pre-nationalization designs, but the British Railway Traffic & Electric Company's 37 t glw hopper, introduced in 1965, broke entirely new ground. Eventually totalling 300 wagons, this fleet comprised four separate batches: BRT 7500-7614 built by Pressed Steel in 1965–6; BRT 7615-7644 and BRT 7645-7744 built by Powell Duffryn in 1967 and 1968; and BRT 7745-7799 built by BREL Doncaster in 1971. All were vacuum braked with Accelerator Freight Inshot being fitted from BRT 7645, earlier batches being modified to AFI in 1967. Accelerator Freight Inshot is a braking distributor designed to operate faster than the normal

vacuum brake and so prevent disruptive reactions between vehicles of a long train which could otherwise lead to broken couplings. It found favour in the 1960s particularly for tank wagon construction, but its development was overtaken by the introduction of air-braked vehicles. BR Double-link suspension was fitted to the first three batches of BRTE hoppers which had a capacity of 24 t, while the final batch were amongst the first wagons to receive English Friction Pedestal suspension units, and were downrated to $23\frac{1}{2}$ t to improve their ride characteristics at high speed.

The hopper body, which was sharply angled to facilitate gravity discharge through a single central hopper situated between the wheels, carried two end-ladders for access to the four hinged loading-hatches in the roof. Slight dimensional variations occur between batches, while for the final two the number of vertical ribs on the hopper side were reduced from eight to five. All were initially hired by the Distillers Group and carried malted barley, used in whisky distilling, from East Anglia and Lincolnshire to Scotland. For many years these wagons were made very conspicuous by the large advertising panels portraying the Group's whisky brands that were carried on their sides, as well as for their distinctive blue livery which gave rise to the nickname 'Blues', although in fact a handful were painted yellow and others brown.

After withdrawal in 1983 when the Distillers Company acquired its own bogie Polybulk wagons (see below), the Powell Duffryn-built 'Blues' were scrapped, but most of the Pressed Steel batch received a top-hatch modification and were transferred to the north-east to carry imported alumina between Blyth and Fort William. Furthermore, 35 of the final batch were given a general refurbishment by Procor, involving re-springing and the fitting of air

BRT 7746, a 37 t bulk grain hopper, stored out of use at Stoke in May 1987. Bodywork is blue with red, black and white 'BRT' symbol, black underframe and white lettering. Note the fixing brackets for the advertisement panels which were originally carried.

brakes, and returned to grain traffic in 1984 on hire to Traffic Services Ltd. They supplement TSL's own Polybulk wagons in general 'Grainflow' traffic and are a particularly common sight at Birkenhead where they supply two flour mills. To correspond with the Polybulks, they are painted in the same green livery with grey ends, top-hatches and solebars, yellow lettering, and black running gear. By 1987, a number had been fitted with a through vacuum pipe and transferred to Blyth to supplement the alumina fleet.

The Procor-built hoppers, PR 14152–14175, were originally classed as aggregate wagons but appear to have seen little use apart from the first four which were hired by the Derwent Valley Railway, a private line near York, for grain traffic, after being fitted with top covers to keep the load dry. By 1981 this line had closed and the remaining 20 had also been rebuilt as covered hoppers by the fitting of weathertight top-doors, reached by a single end-ladder, and at the same time were recoded

PAA and uprated from 30 t to 35 t capacity. All have three pneumatically-operated sets of hopper doors and BSC Friction Pedestal suspension with an unusually long 20 ft wheelbase.

The first four conversions were hired to Steetley Minerals for lime traffic out of Hindlow, Derbyshire, before being moved to the north-east in 1987 to carry potash, while the remaining 20 vehicles were sold to ICI's Agricultural Division and carry urea, a granulated chemical used in the production of resins, from ICI's plant at Haverton Hill to the Ciba-Geigy works at Duxford in Cambridgeshire. The original orange livery is still carried by PR 14152–14155, the rest having been repainted dark green with a white ICI symbol and lettering and their number prefix changed to ICIA.

Lime hoppers, two-axle

Five of the two-axle covered hopper types are used for carrying lime, generally for the steel and glass-making industries, and their designs reflect the technical developments and increased capacities which have been such a feature of the private wagon scene in recent years. Firstly are two batches of 46 t glw vehicles built by Standard Wagon in 1970 and 1972, the only difference being the fitting of BSC Friction Pedestal suspension and the lack of a through pipe on the BRTE vehicles. All have a distinctive curved body with sloping ends and two discharge hoppers, loading being through three hinged roof-hatches reached by two end-ladders and a catwalk running the full length of the wagon side. A number of the Procor batch have been modified to carry alumina, four circular fillers replacing the three hinged covers, but the majority are still in lime traffic for Steetley Minerals. The 69 BRTE lime hoppers are all hired to British Steel, Teesside, and run between Hardendale Quarry, near Shap, and the blast furnaces at Lackenby and Redcar.

Built in 1974, the British Steel, Glasgow, lime hoppers are to a more advanced design with a much longer wheelbase at 20 ft 3 in, as against 16 ft on the earlier vehicles. The body is supported along each side by six struts, and can carry 37 t. In place of separate loading hatches they are fitted with a full-length top-opening with a one-piece hinged roof cover which allows for quicker loading, while at the same time reducing the risk of water contamination. BSC Friction Pedestal suspension is fitted, and the type operates exclusively between Hardendale Quarry and the Ravenscraig steel complex near Motherwell.

British Steel, Ravenscraig, also owned a fleet of covered hoppers built by Procor and BREL Shildon in 1979. They were dual-purpose vehicles, coded PGA, and capable of carrying a 38 t load of directly-reduced iron pellets, although they could also be used to carry lime, being equipped with air-operated parallelogram top-doors to protect such a load. They were intended to operate to Ravenscraig, carrying iron ore pellets from Hunterston and lime from Hardendale, but seem to have spent most of their short life stored out of use until being withdrawn in 1984.

Built by Standard Wagon in 1981 for block-train operation between Thrislington Quarry, Co Durham, and the Steetley

---

PR 8035 is one of a number of these distinctively-shaped covered hoppers which have been modified for alumina traffic. Livery is grey body, heavily weathered, with blue and black lettering on white patches and black underframe. Horbury, May 1986 (T. Mann).

Steetley Refractories owns a modern fleet of covered hoppers fitted with Gloucester Floating-axle suspension and air-operated top-cover. Also prominent are the metal side-panels which facilitate movement by Hymid Wagon Controllers. The off-white overall livery, common to many of the lime-carrying types, is enhanced in the case of STET 18703 by a white nameboard with black lettering. Tees Yard, September 1987.

Chemicals plant near Hartlepool, Steetley Refractories' 30 lime hoppers are similar to the earlier Standard build in that they have a curved, steeply-angled body. However, neither ladders nor catwalks is necessary as the Steetley fleet is fitted with air-operated parallelogram top-covers operated from ground level. Large metal plates are fixed to each side of the hopper body to facilitate shunting by ground-based Hymid Wagon Controllers, while the 19 ft wheelbase underframe is fitted with Gloucester Floating axle suspension. Carrying capacity is 36 t.

Other covered hoppers, two-axle

The four remaining types of covered hopper wagon listed in Table 4 are all highly specialized designs. Alcan owns 19 32 t capacity, unfitted hoppers, used for carrying alumina, a fine powder used in the production of aluminium, between the import berth at Blyth and their works at Lynemouth. These wagons, which can also carry petroleum coke, were built by BREL Ashford in 1971 and resemble an enlarged

British Railways 'Covhop'. They have BR Friction-link suspension but continuous brakes were not considered necessary as they are restricted to working entirely over freight-only lines.

Built the previous year at BREL's Doncaster works, the 17 BRTE 46 t glw petroleum coke hoppers were one of the first types to be fitted with Gloucester Friction Pedestal suspension. Hired to Anglesey Aluminium, they work as a block train between Conoco's Humber Oil Refinery, Immingham, and Holyhead, where the coke is used in the electrolysis of alumina. The hopper body has a unique angular shape to take advantage of the settling properties of the coke, with four small roof-hatches, end-ladders, and full-length catwalks. Discharge of the 33 t load is via two gravity-fed hoppers situated between the wheels.

The eight $37\frac{1}{2}$ t two-axle china clay hoppers owned by Tiger Rail Leasing and hired to Tullis Russell, have a high narrow body fitted with a one-piece, centre-weighted, sliding roof-cover and two discharge hoppers. In their design, account

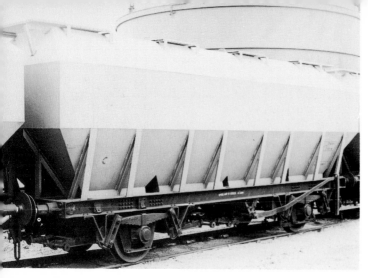

One of the small batch of unfitted covered hoppers, ALCN 12025, recorded at Blyth Docks in August 1981. Bodywork is grey with black lettering; underframe black with white lettering. Unusually, the number panel is painted on the right-hand end of the body (R. Silsbury).

The angular shape of the BRTE petroleum coke hoppers is well illustrated in this view of BRT 12100, taken at Horbury in April 1986. Livery is overall black with white lettering. Both the 'Procor' symbol, in blue and white, and the 'BRT' symbol in red, black and white are carried, along with the Anglesey Aluminium 'Double-Teardrop' device in red and blue on white patches, the latter almost entirely obscured beneath the grime (T. Mann).

TRL 12801, one of the eight china clay hoppers operated by Tullis Russell. The attractive livery comprises blue bodywork, black underframe and white lettering. 'Tullis Russell The Papermakers' is in blue on a white panel, whereas the 'TRL' insignia comprises black and maroon symbols and black lettering on a yellow panel. Crewe, July 1987.

had to be taken of the restricted clearances available on the short branch to the Tullis Russell paper mill at Markinch, hence the adoption of a 16 ft wheelbase so as to negotiate the curvature on the line. Gloucester Floating-axle suspension is fitted to allow them to operate in Speedlink services between Cornwall and Markinch.

High-grade sand, for use in glassmaking, is carried by the 38 t covered hoppers owned by British Industrial Sand, which were built by W.H. Davis and Standard Wagon in 1981–2 to replace life-expired British Railways' wagons on workings from the sand quarries at Middleton Towers, near Kings Lynn. Both batches feature a sloping hopper body, supported by four flying-buttress-like struts along each side, and a large angle plate at each end, suitable for both dry and wet sand. Such a robust design serves to prevent distortion of the hopper body, while the angle plates at each end also protect the air cylinder used to power the top-cover and bottom doors. Each wagon has two sets of pneumatically-operated hopper doors, with loading through the full-length opening in the top. The Davis-built wagons have a one-piece hinged top-cover, but the Standard-built vehicles are fitted with two-piece parallelogram top-covers, this being the only noticeable difference between the

two batches. A 16 ft wheelbase is common to all, along with Gloucester Floating-axle suspension.

The type has proved very successful in handling what is a notoriously difficult commodity, and as well as operating between Kings Lynn and Yorkshire they also serve glassworks in the St Helens area bringing sand from Oakamoor, near Stoke-on-Trent. In 1982, BIS 7957 lost its roof, to be followed by a further five such conversions in 1987. All six wagons were recoded PGA and allocated to sand traffic between Redhill, Sussex, and the Crosfields chemical plant at Warrington, Cheshire.

Covered hoppers, bogie

Covered hopper bogie wagons are somewhat less common than their four-wheeled counterparts. The first variant, listed in Table 5, is the fleet of 63 t, gravity load and discharge hoppers built by Charles Roberts in 1972 for the wagon hire company Storage & Transport Systems, and hired to Cleveland Potash to carry muriate of potash from its mine at Boulby, on the North Yorkshire coast, to Tees Dock. They have an all-welded, mild steel body, with a full-length top-filling hatch and four sets of bottom discharge doors. The underframe is also of all-welded construction with

BIS 7957 was built as a covered hopper but seen here at Warrington in September 1987 it had lost its top cover and been recoded PGA. The bodywork is white with black lettering, orange 'BIS' symbol and stripe; the underframe is black with white lettering.

Table 5: *Covered hopper wagons, bogie*

Type	Number series		TOPS code	Builder	Date	Owner/Operator
Potash	STS	11401–11434	PBA	Charles Roberts	1972	STS/Cleveland Potash
Tripolyphosphate	CL	84701	TEB	Charles Roberts	1969	City Leasing/P & G
Tripolyphosphate	PR	11300–11312	PBA	Charles Roberts	1972	Procor/various
China clay	TRL	11600–11634	PBA	Fauvet Girel	1982	Tiger Rail/ECC
Cement clinker	RLS	11800–11815	PBA	Standard Wagon	1982	Railease/Clyde Cement
General purpose	TRL	13500–13524	PBA	Cadoux	1982	Tiger Rail/various
Grain/china clay	33 70 9382 000–064		PIB	Fauvet Girel	1974	Traffic Services Ltd
Grain	33 70 9385 000–029		PIB	Fauvet Girel	1981	TSL/Grainflow
Grain	33 70 9280 030–081		PIA	Fauvet Girel	1983–4	TSL/Grainflow
Grain	33 70 9280 000–029		PIA	CFMF France	1983	Scottish Malt Distillers
Grain	33 70 9382 100–129		PIA	Fauvet Girel	1984	STS
Powders	33 70 9292 201–215		PIA	Arbel Fauvet	1987	Tiphook Rail

Gloucester '3-piece Fastfreight' bogies. Body livery is mid-green with white ends and top-cover, white lettering and Cleveland Potash symbol. In addition to block-train workings to Tees Dock, these wagons also run in Speedlink services to destinations in Scotland and East Anglia.

Charles Roberts also built the 13 71 t bulk powder vehicles, intended for sodium tripolyphosphate traffic between White-haven and the Proctor & Gamble factory at West Thurrock, on the Thames estuary. The revolutionary design, which had been tested in a prototype wagon, CL 84701, some three years previously, comprised a specially shaped barrel-like body, having a cylindrical centre section with offset conical frustrum sections at each end to take full advantage of the settlement properties of the load. Filling pipework was provided at each end, the access hatches on top of the barrel being for use in an emergency or when cleaning out the inside. An all-welded underframe carried the complicated discharge gear comprising four air-assisted hoppers, with the then new Gloucester GPS 25 bogies fitted, for a top speed of 60 mph. Livery was originally a pale green body with two white vertical bands, and black Proctor & Gamble symbol, solebars and bogies.

In 1977, the prototype, which had been erroneously coded as a tank, was written off in a serious derailment on the Cumbrian Coast line along with five other wagons, PR 11301/2/3/7/10, after which the remainder were gradually withdrawn from use. However, in 1986 all eight survivors received a further lease of life when they were refurbished by Procor for hire to the Corn Products Company, to carry powdered starch from Manchester to paper mills in Scotland and the South-east.

Tiger Rail introduced its first bogie covered hoppers in 1982 as a replacement for British Rail's obsolescent 12½ t china clay opens. Designed and developed in conjunction with English China Clay International and built by French hopper specialists, Etablissements Fauvet Girel, these 56 t capacity vehicles have proved a great success. The body is profiled to allow for front loading by shovel, as normally practised at ECC's drying plants, without loss of payload, and a bi-directional waterproof cover is fitted for the top-hatch. A dead-fall system with snap-over arch-breaker arms, similar to those found in modern coal hoppers, has been fitted so that the wagons can transport not only the dried 'lump' clay but also the far stickier 'ball' clay, which is produced by ECC's Devon works. The wagons ride on French Y25 CS2 bogies and can average $2\frac{1}{2}$ loaded journeys per week between the West Country and the Potteries. Internally, these wagons have a high-quality finish to protect the china clay from contamination, while externally the body and solebar are painted white. Lettering and a horizontal stripe are blue, with black top-cover and bogies.

The second batch of Tiger-owned wagons listed in Table 5 are also French built, comprising 25 general purpose vehicles built by Cadoux. The all-welded body, which is unusually fitted with a detachable roof, has a curved profile which takes full advantage of the restrictive British loading gauge to give an impressive 66 t payload within a gross laden weight of only 88 t. The hogsback hopper design minimizes internal compartment division of the three hoppers which are each fitted with pneumatic doors to assist rapid discharge of difficult products. Livery comprises a lime green body and solebar, while the Y25 CSM bogies are black. Lettering is white with the 'Tiger' wording in yellow and black. This design has also proved a success, and despite their small number they can be seen throughout the country carrying such diverse loads as coal, sugarstone, agricultural lime, petroleum coke, and calcified seaweed.

In marked contrast, the Railease fleet of 88 t covered hoppers was designed solely for the carriage of cement clinker and is therefore more restricted in its operation. The vehicles' slab-sided body profile, with three top-filling hatches, provides a $63\frac{1}{2}$ t payload for this heavy product, which is gravity discharged through three sets of

Following a slump in cement clinker traffic, many Railease covered bogie hoppers were stored at various locations in the North-west and a number have subsequently been modified with cut-down sides. However, RLS 11800 remained in original condition when photographed at Blackburn in May 1987. Livery is white bodywork with pale green and dark blue stripes and black lettering. Solebars and bogies are dark green with white lettering.

bottom doors. French Y25 CSM bogies are also fitted to these wagons, which were the first single-pipe air-braked vehicles built in the UK to operate on British Rail.

The entire fleet is hired to Clyde Cement and operates between Clitheroe, Lancashire, and Coatbridge, near Glasgow, although a slump in traffic saw many stored out of use by the end of 1986. Those still in use are gradually being uprated to carry $65\frac{1}{2}$ t as well as undergoing a programme of door modification.

Polybulks

Trade between Britain and Europe has grown in importance in recent years, particularly since Britain joined the European Economic Community in 1973, and a significant proportion travels in railway wagons via the train ferry services. Until 1987, two routes were available, but in February of that year the Harwich–Zeebrugge route closed, all sailings being thenceforth concentrated on the Dover–Dunkerque link.

Only vehicles numbered in accordance with the UIC (Union International de Chemin de Fers) 12-digit system, and registered as part of the *RIV* (Regolamento Internationale Veicili), the organization set up to regulate international freight workings, are allowed to run on the continent, while vehicles intended for operation to and from Britain via the train ferries must also be fitted with chaining-down lugs to facilitate stowage on the boat.

The majority of such vehicles that visit Britain are registered abroad, and therefore outside the scope of this book, but a number of types are British-registered, one of the most significant in terms of wagon design being the Polybulk bogie covered hopper, the first batch of which arrived in 1974.

These 80 t glw, all-steel vehicles were an important advance for the time, being

A number of the TSL-owned Polybulks have changed hands, including 33 70 9382 003–9, recorded at Kings Lynn in July 1987 when being loaded with urea. The bodywork is a mixture of green and grey; bogies and hopper discharge doors are black, and all lettering white. Interestingly, this wagon carried round-headed buffers at the other end.

Built by Fauvet Girel in 1983, 33 70 9280 049-5 illustrates the increased length of the Grainflow polybulk wagons. The colourful livery comprises green body sides with light grey roof, ends and underframe. The 'Grainflow' letter and 'ear of corn' symbol are yellow, and the 'TSL' emblem red, black and white. Other lettering is white on the body, black along the solebar. Wallasey, May 1987.

capable of carrying a 58 t load, and an initial 65 wagons, owned by Traffic Services, were allocated to a lucrative two-way traffic. This involved a weekly 22–24 wagon train-load of pelletized china clay, originating roughly half in Devon, half in Cornwall, which was destined for Bibirist, Switzerland. The return working conveyed imported grain to a storage depot at Pinhoe, near Exeter, although as Britain's grain harvest increased, this half of the traffic ceased in 1977.

However, it has been in the transportation of grain within the UK that the French-built Polybulk wagons have made the greatest impact. Traffic Services introduced a second batch in 1981, similar in basic outline to the earlier vehicles but dedicated to the 'Grainflow' service, a joint marketing venture with British Rail, designed to secure a substantial share of the rapidly expanding UK grain production for rail transport. By 1983, when a further batch of 'Grainflow' Polybulks was brought into use, some 230,000 t of grain had been gathered on to rail, largely on workings within Britain, but also including the occasional wagon-load of malted barley for export.

Encouraged by the success of the Polybulk wagons within the 'Grainflow' operation, and with British Rail's improved performance following the introduction of Speedlink, the Distillers Group, who had become increasingly dissatisfied with their leased fleet of mechanically out-

Similar in outline to the Polybulk wagons is this Tiphook powder hopper, 33 70 9292 203–4, seen at Crewe in December 1987 when part of the Tiphook Rail Freight Exhibition Train. The body is pale grey with black lettering; solebars and underframe fittings are blue and bogies black. The 'Tiphook' logo is orange and blue on a white panel.

dated, uneconomically-sized wagons, purchased their own fleet of 30 Polybulks in 1983. Finally, in 1984 Storage and Transport Systems introduced a further 30 vehicles for the transport of imported grain derivatives and substitutes, such as rape seed and tapioca, from a terminal at New Holland on the south bank of the Humber. Although resembling the earlier Polybulks, these $57\frac{1}{2}$ t hoppers have a modified discharge arrangement to suit the transported product's characteristics. Both the Distillers and STS Polybulks carry very distinctive liveries; the former sports an attractive white and blue striped colour scheme, with yellow and black lettering, while the latter are painted bright orange with red and black lettering.

The 15 powder wagons owned by Tiphook Rail began trial running in 1987. They are twin-compartment, 90 t glw covered hoppers, and are suitable for a wide range of commodities including such traffics as alumina, basic slag, pulverized coal, and starch. Their expected use, as with the entire Tiphook Rail fleet, is to be on the short-term spot-hire traffic flows.

Chapter 3

Bulk Powder Wagons

Some years before the 1955 Modernization Plan, British Railways had identified powdered materials as a potential growth area for its freight business. In 1954, following a considerable period of development, the Presflo wagon was introduced, a revolutionary new design specifically for the carriage of powders in bulk.

Although suitable for a wide range of powders, the Presflo was primarily intended for products such as cement which tend to compact whilst in transit, thus making discharge difficult, so while being gravity loaded through two roof-hatches, compressed air was used to assist discharge. To prevent distortion when being discharged, the wagon body was reinforced by a grid of horizontal and vertical ribs, giving the vehicle a most distinctive appearance. The prototype was vacuum braked, with shoe suspension and a 10 ft 6 in wheelbase; it carried 20 t, uprated to $22\frac{1}{2}$ t in the production batch which quickly followed as all the cement industry majors began to adopt the type for block-train operation.

Table 6: *Bulk cement wagons, two-axle, vacuum braked*

Type	Number series	TOPS code	Builder	Date	Owner/Operator
Presflo	TC 8951–8958	PCV	Butterley	1960	Tunnel Cement
Presflo	APCM 8601–8828	PCV	Various	1960–3	Associated Portland Cement
Cemflo	APCM 8301–8490	PCV	Gloucester RC & W	1961–2	Associated Portland Cement
Cemflo	APCM 8500–8594	PCV	Metro-Cammell	1963–6	Associated Portland Cement
Powders	ALG 9080–9099	PCF	Interconsult, Sweden	1965	Algeco/APCM

Bulk cement wagons, two-axle, vacuum-braked

In 1960, the Associated Portland Cement Manufacturing Company — later to become known as Blue Circle Industries — introduced its own fleet of Presflos, built by Butterley and Metro Cammell, as a direct copy of the British Railways design. Originally the main body colour was yellow, but as this soon became overlaid with cement dust, it was changed to light grey with black lettering; the underframe

The first modern private owner wagons for bulk cement were direct copies of the BR Presflo design. APCM 8700, recorded at Radstock in 1974, illustrates this type. The bodywork is light grey with black underframe, and black lettering on yellow patches. The nameplate is yellow with blue main lettering, blue circle with white lettering and centre, and 'Snowcrete' brand in white on red patches (D. Larkin).

remained black with white lettering. These wagons were a common sight, operating in company with the railway-owned versions to Blue Circle depots throughout the country until their replacement by air-braked vehicles began in 1984.

Tunnel Cement also purchased eight identical vacuum-braked Presflos from Butterley in 1960, which were used for many years to carry special cement from the works at Aberthaw in South Wales. Livery comprised bauxite bodywork with white lettering, and a black underframe. A large red nameplate, painted with a white 'T' and 'TUNNEL BULK CEMENT' in black was fixed to the body side, although the majority had lost this namplate by 1987 when they were withdrawn.

The problem of incomplete discharge,

caused by powder lodging in the corners of the Presflo's angular body, resulted in the introduction of a second vacuum-braked design by APCM in 1961. The Cemflo, or 'LA' as it became known, differed markedly from the previous type in having a cylindrical aluminium alloy vessel which was fitted with a simplified air-assisted discharge, so had no need of a heavily reinforced construction. Coupled with the increased length, the design provided for a one-third improvement in payload-to-tare ratio, and the 'LAs' were introduced on a new block-train working from Cliffe, Kent, to Uddingston, near Glasgow. Between 1961 and 1965, some 285 'LAs' were built, initially by the Gloucester Railway Carriage & Wagon Company with eyebolt suspension, and later by Metro Cammell with Double-link suspension. However, in 1967 a serious derailment at Thirsk brought into question their stability, and despite a series of suspension modifications they were eventually transferred to northern England to operate shorter-haul services. Their standard light grey livery was originally enhanced by a small circular Blue Circle nameplate in blue and yellow. In 1984, APCM 8566 was air braked and fitted with Double-link taperleaf suspension, but no more were to be so modified as Blue Circle decided to invest in brand new air-braked wagons.

In an attempt to overcome the ride problems associated with the 'LAs', APCM hired a small number of 46 t glw powder wagons from Algeco. Built in Sweden by Interconsult, Falkenburg, they were similar to the 'LAs' but with a more bulbous end to the vessel, which was also carried higher on the underframe. Double-link suspension,

with a 15 ft wheelbase, was retained, and these wagons remained in use until 1983. As well as the standard light grey Blue Circle livery, they also carried an orange and black 'Algeco' panel, located centrally on the side of the barrel.

Blue Circle bulk cement wagons, two-axle, air-braked

In the mid-1960s, APCM introduced two prototype air-braked Presflos, APCM 9025, the first of the now familiar 'Chevron' or 'depressed-centre' type, and APCM 9020, which owed much to oil tank design of the period. Although the latter design could boast a slightly greater payload, only four more were to be constructed before APCM decided to concentrate on the 'depressed-centre' type,

The 'LA' or Cemflo cement wagons remained in use in the North-west when this view of APCM 8522 was taken at Ditton in September 1987. It carried the common APCM livery of grey body with black lettering and underframe.

Table 7: *Blue Circle bulk cement wagons, two-axle, air-braked*

Type	Number series	TOPS code	Builder	Date	Owner/Operator
Presflo	APCM 9020–9024	PCB	Standard Wagon	1967–9	Associated Portland Cement
Presflo	APCM 9025–9075	PCB	Metro Cammell	1966–9	Associated Portland Cement
Presflo	APCM 9100–9399	PCA	BREL Various	1973–4	Associated Portland Cement
Presflo	APCM 9425–9434	PCA	BREL Doncaster	1974	Associated Portland Cement
Presflo	APCM 10700–10837	PCA	BREL Various	1979–81	Associated Portland Cement
Presflo	APCM 10838	PCA	CFMF, France	1980	Associated Portland Cement
Presflo	BCC 10839–10849	PCA	CFMF, France	1981	Blue Circle Cement
Presflo	BCC 10850–10987	PCA	Various	1981	Blue Circle Cement
Metalair	BCC 10667–10699	PCA	Powell Duffryn	1984–5	Blue Circle Cement
Metalair	BCC 10988–11141	PCA	Various	1984–6	Blue Circle Cement

which featured a specially shaped, single-compartment barrel, which sloped inwards towards the central discharge outlet, facilitating discharge.

Following an initial batch of 51 such wagons, built between 1966 and 1969, a further 586 were constructed up until 1981, all to a slightly larger 38½ t design with a 16 ft wheelbase and Gloucester Floating-axle suspension. Both the 1979 batch, APCM 10700–10837 built at BREL's Ashford and Shildon works, and the 1981 batch, BCC 10850–10987 built by Procor and Standard Wagon, were fitted with Hermann aeration equipment for rapid pressure discharge into overhead silos, as well as a gravity-fed bot-

---

APCM 9227 is an early example of the 'depressed-centre' Presflo being built at Doncaster in 1974. Livery is light grey and black, with black lettering, some on white patches. Northenden, December 1987.

Successor to the 'depressed-centre' type is the 'Metalair' design, illustrated in this view of BCC 11050 at Heywood in November 1985. The livery remained grey and black. At the time of this photograph, a temporary cement terminal had been established at Heywood while Northenden underwent modernization.

tom outlet for unloading between the rails, thus allowing operation to any site in the country. All the 'depressed-centre' Presflos received standard light grey livery, though since 1970 none has carried the Blue Circle nameplates.

In 1984, Blue Circle, in collaboration with wagon builders Powell Duffryn and powder tank specialists Metalair, developed a new, light-weight barrel allowing a higher payload and faster discharge than previous 51 t glw designs. APCM 9124 was fitted with the new barrel and re-numbered BCC 10988, to be followed by the first production batch, BCC 10667–10699, later in 1984. With governmental assistance, Blue Circle subsequently purchased a further 153 Metalair wagons to replace their ageing vacuum-braked fleet, all having a 16 ft 3¼ in wheelbase with Gloucester Floating-axle suspension.

Storage & Transport Systems, together with French wagon builders CFMF, also developed a 51 t glw cement wagon for Blue Circle, numbered APCM 10838. This design featured steeply-sloping ends, similar to a covered hopper, and carried 'powderjet fluidization equipment' to assist discharge, but although another 11 were purchased in 1981, Blue Circle decided to concentrate on the 'Metalair' concept.

Other bulk cement wagons, two-axle, air-braked

In addition to their eight vacuum-braked Presflos, Tunnel Cement also purchased a large fleet of air-braked wagons for use on services from its plant at Tring to depots in London and Southampton. Built by Installation Manufacturing Contractors, Hartlepool, they were the first 16 ft wheel-

Table 8: *Other bulk cement wagons, two-axle, air-braked*

Type	Number series		TOPS code	Builder	Date	Owner/Operator
Presflo	TC	8983–9018	PCA	Installation MC	1972–3	Tunnel Cement
Presflo	TC	9490–9493	PCA	Standard Wagon	1977	Tunnel Cement
Presflo	RBL	10400–10443	PCA	Standard Wagon	1977	Ribblesdale Cement
Presflo	RLS	10300–10344	PCA	Standard Wagon	1983	Railease/Tunnel Cement
Presflo	PR	9400–9424	PCA	Charles Roberts	1973–4	Procor/Rugby Cement
Presflo	ML	9435–9459	PCA	Procor	1975	Mercantile Leasing/Rugby Cement
Presflo	ML	10019–10024	PCA	Procor	1975	Mercantile Leasing/Rugby Cement
Presflo	PR	10025–10049	PCA	Procor	1981	Procor/Rugby Cement
Presflo	RC	10050–10064	PCA	Procor	1984–5	Rugby Cement
Presflo	TRL	9460–9474	PCA	BREL Doncaster	1975	Tiger Rail/Ketton Cement
Presflo	TRL	10500–10521	PCA	BREL Ashford	1977	Tiger Rail/various
Presflo	TRL	10534–10539	PCA	Standard Wagon	1981	Tiger Rail/Ketton Cement
Presflo	STS	10600–10651	PCA	CFMF, France	1982–3	STS/various
Presflo	STS	74030–74044	PCA	Fauvet Girel	1985	STS/Rugby Cement
Twin Cone	23 70 9192 002		PIA	Ateliers, France	1985	STS/Tunnel Cement
Twin Cone	43 70 9192 003–022		PIA	Ateliers, France	1986	STS/Tunnel Cement

base powder wagons with BSC Friction Pedestal suspension and dual discharge gear. Body livery is red with a white company symbol and lettering, except for 'TUNNEL CEMENT' which is in black.

In 1977, Standard Wagon built four additional Presflos for Tunnel Cement to a slightly modified design, followed by a large

RBL 10434 illustrates the revised livery style applied to these wagons in 1981 with a smaller 'Castle' symbol. In common with the Tunnel Cement PCAs, these vehicles are fitted with two discharge pipes and English Steel pedestal suspension. Heywood, December 1987.

fleet for Tunnel's associate company Ribblesdale Cement. The Ribblesdale fleet operates from Clitheroe to depots in the North-east, and originally carried a most attractive light grey livery which featured a prominent 'castle' symbol in red on a white ground, with black lettering and green solebars. Standard Wagon also constructed a third batch to the same basic design in 1983, but with Gloucester Floating-axle suspension, and without the end-ladder or catwalks fitted to the two previous batches. All are hired to Tunnel Cement and work from Penyffordd, near Wrexham, to depots in the Midlands and North Wales.

Charles Roberts also designed an air-braked bulk powder wagon, fitted with their own 'pressure-flow' discharge system. Loading could be accomplished either through three top-hatches, reached by end-ladders and full-length catwalks, or via a bottom filler situated beneath the solebar, thus enabling filling from road vehicles. The first batch were built in 1973 for hire to Rugby Cement, to be followed by a further three batches from Procor, some of which

were originally leased to Rugby Cement by Mercantile Leasing, a holding company, before being sold outright in 1983. The first batch originally carried a green livery, but by 1985 all were in Rugby's light grey livery, with black and red lettering and a black company symbol. Procor has also built an interesting variant on the original Charles Roberts design in which the floor of the barrel slopes inwards towards the centre, similar to a 'depressed-centre' type Presflo. All 15 are owned by Rugby Cement and work from the cement works at Foxton to depots in East Anglia and the south.

The Tiger Rail Presflos listed in Table 8 are all to the standard 16 ft wheelbase 'depressed-centre' design, the Doncaster-built wagons being fitted with Gloucester Pedestal suspension, the remainder with BSC Friction Pedestal. All are now hired to Ketton Cement and are painted green, although TRL 10500–10518 have a much paler green livery than the others as they were originally hired to Lytag for a short-term movement of fly-ash from Didcot

As detailed in the text, the Railease PCAs lack an end-ladder and are fitted with Gloucester Floating-axle suspension. When photographed at Warrington in September 1987, RLS 10309 still carried its original livery comprising a grey tank with red 'Tunnel Cement' lettering largely obscured beneath cement dust, and a black underframe, although many of this batch had been repainted for Castle Cement.

Cement wagons are difficult to keep clean, hence their often rather drab liveries. This problem is highlighted with TRL 9460, seen at Wymondham in July 1987. Underneath the cement the basic livery is light green with black lettering and underframe.

Power Station to Tilbury.

Since the sale of a dozen 'powderjet' type Presflos to Blue Circle Cement in 1980–81, STS have introduced two further batches of these vehicles, one for general spot-hire, the other for Rugby Cement traffic out of Halling, Kent. Both batches are identical in design to the earlier wagons with Gloucester Pedestal suspension and a 16 ft wheelbase, although the third batch, numbered unusually in the 74xxx series, carries Rugby Cement's light grey livery.

The only type of two-axle bulk powder ferry wagons to be British registered are also owned by STS. These are the 40 t glw 'Twin Cone' vehicles built by Ateliers de Joigney, France, using redundant underframes taken from old French wagons. Reminiscent of the British Railways Prestwin design, they carry 29 t of cement and are hired to Tunnel Cement to work between Tring and Southampton.

Other bulk powder wagons, two-axle

Although cement is by far the most important powder in terms of quantity to be carried by rail, there are also a handful of chemical powders that are so transported. Of these, sodium carbonate, or soda ash as it is more commonly known, is of particular significance, being used in both the glass-making and detergent industries.

Until 1976, a fleet of 45 t glw vacuum-braked wagons, owned by STS and leased to ICI Mond, carried soda ash from Northwich to Scotland. The first two wagons, STS 53400–53401, built by Herederos de Ramon Mugica, were fitted with through air pipes, a refinement omitted from the remainder, all being similar to standard oil tank wagons apart from the distinctive discharge gear and four top-fillers. Livery comprised a blue barrel with white lettering

Table 9: *Other bulk powder wagons, two-axle*

Type	Number series		TOPS code	Builder	Date	Owner/Operator
Soda ash	STS	53400–53401	PCW	H de RM, Spain	1966	STS/ICI Mond
Soda ash	STS	53402–53426	PCV	Pressed Steel	1966	STS/ICI Mond
Soda ash	PR	9475–9489	PCA	Procor	1976–7	Procor/ICI Mond
Soda ash	PR	10100–10124	PCA	Procor	1980–81	Procor/ICI Mond
Powders	PR	10000–10018	PCA	Procor	1975–6	Procor/various
Tripoly-phosphate	PR	9494–9499	PCA	Procor	1983	Procor/Albright & Wilson
Tripoly-phosphate	PR	10125–10134	PCA	Procor	1983–4	Procor/Albright & Wilson
Tripoly-phosphate	TRL	10522–10533	PCA	Standard Wagon	1981	Tiger Rail/Lever Bros
Soda ash/Barytes	TRL	10540–10569	PCA	BREL Shildon	1983	Tiger Rail/various
Tip-Air	RLS	12200–12259	TTA*	Standard Wagon	1974	Railease/ICI Mond
Alumina	BACO	55531–55573†	PCA	Powell Duffryn	1987–8	British Aluminium

* RLS 12200 originally coded TTB. In 1981 the entire fleet of Tip-Air wagons was recoded 'PE'.

† Series re-prefixed BAHS, 'British Aluminium Highland Smelter', in 1988.

Right *Two beautifully clean Presflos owned by Procor and hired to ICI Mond for sodium carbonate are seen in Oakleigh Sidings, Northwich, in October 1987. The vehicle nearest the camera, PR 10107, was built in 1980 and carries an overall white livery with black lettering.*

Below right *When comparing this view of PR 10013, taken at West Thurrock in 1980, with the previous illustration, various detail differences may be noted between these two batches of 'pressure-flow' Presflos. Most notable is the lack of catwalks on PR 10013 which was then on hire to Proctor & Gamble and carried a bright green body livery, with white lettering on black patches and black underframe with white lettering* (D. Larkin).

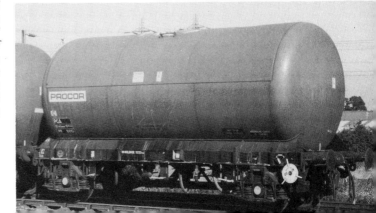

and black underframe. They were replaced by air-braked Presflos, built by Procor to the same 'pressure-flow' design as had been used for the Rugby Cement fleet.

The same 'pressure-flow' design was used for the batch of 19 Presflos, PR 10000–10018, introduced in 1975. This batch was something of a mixed bag in that nine wagons were standard and intended for cement or soda ash traffic, while the others, which were built without ladders and with only one top-filler, were hired to Proctor & Gamble to carry sodium tripoly-phosphate between Whitehaven and West Thurrock. However, they were not a complete success in this traffic and by 1986 all were being converted to carry cement or else put into store, Procor in the meantime having introduced a 'depressed-centre' type Presflo more suitable for tripoly-phosphate.

Although allocated two separate number series, the vehicles in this batch, built in 1983 and 1984, are all identical with Her-mann aeration equipment and bottom fillers, being hired to Albright & Wilson rather than Proctor & Gamble. The bottom filler permits loading from road vehicles, a feature which became essential in 1987 following closure of the rope-worked incline up to the Albright & Wilson works in Whitehaven.

Tiger Rail also owns a small number of 'depressed-centre' Presflos used for tripoly-phosphate traffic from Whitehaven. Identical to Tiger's cement-carrying Presflos apart from the addition of a bottom filler, these wagons are painted in a colourful mauve livery and run to the Lever Brothers soap works in Warrington.

The final batch of Tiger Presflos, built at Shildon in 1983, differ from earlier 'depressed-centre' types in having a conical end-vessel strake. They are equipped for both gravity and pressure discharge, the majority being leased to Rockware Glass to carry heavy soda ash from the ICI works around Northwich to glassworks in

TRL 10556, one of the third batch of Tiger Rail Presflos built for soda ash traffic. The livery is a blue body with yellow lettering and black underframe. Warrington, July 1987.

By October 1987, the entire fleet of Railease 'Tip-Air' wagons was stored out of use, many at Heywood including RLS 12208 seen in this end view showing the hydraulic mechanism used to raise the tank body. Livery is overall off-white with black lettering, and the 'Railease' name is in light blue on a white panel.

Knottingley and Doncaster. Other traffics carried by wagons from this batch include cement and barytes.

In addition to heavy soda ash, ICI also produces a much lighter form of sodium carbonate for use in various chemical processes, particularly soap powder manufacture. To accomplish discharge of this lightweight material, Standard Wagon developed the unique Tip-Air concept, which involved mounting a pressure discharge tank vessel on a specially constructed underframe. The underframe is fitted with a pneumatic ram at one end which allows the tank to be tilted to provide a sloping bed before unloading begins. A fleet of some 60 Tip-Airs were introduced for block-train working between Northwich

and Whitehaven, only the prototype RLS 12200 having a through vacuum pipe. All have BSC Friction Pedestal suspension with a 17 ft wheelbase, and can carry 26 t within a gross laden weight of 43 t. Originally they were coded as 'TTs', but since they do not carry a liquid this was revised to 'PE' in 1981.

Finally in this category there are the 43 51 t glw two-axle powder wagons introduced by British Aluminium in December 1987. Built by Powell Duffryn, they are virtually identical to the 'Metalair'-type cement wagons produced for Blue Circle, and are intended to eventually replace all other vehicle types on the alumina workings from Blyth.

Table 10: *Bulk powder wagons, bogie*

Type	Number series		TOPS code	Builder	Date	Owner/Operator
Cement	APCM	9500–9549	PDA	Metro Cammell	1972	Associated Portland Cement
Cement	LS	9700–9766	PDA	Metro Cammell	1969–72	Lloyds & Scottish/ Blue Circle
Cement	RLS	9800–9835	PDA	Standard Wagon	1982	Railease/Clyde Cement
Cement	RC	11900	PDA	Not known		Rugby Cement

Bogie Presflo BCC 9756 was formerly owned by Lloyds & Scottish and retained that company's black and white 'horse and thistle' emblem when photographed at Coalville in July 1987. Otherwise the livery is standard grey and black. In the background stands RLS 9802, one of the bogie Presflos operated by Clyde Cement.

Bulk powder wagons, bogie

Only two fleets of bogie Presflos have been built, most operators preferring the greater flexibility offered by two-axle vehicles. Each of Blue Circle's fleet of 102 t glw wagons is in effect two two-axle 'depressed-centre' vessels mounted on a 50 ft 10 in long underframe, carried on Gloucester Metalistik Mk 3 bogies. Carrying 79 t and having both gravity and Hermanns pressurized discharge systems for maximum flexibility, they usually operate in block-train formations from Northfleet, Kent, and Hope, Derbyshire. Body livery is grey with black lettering and underframe, all originally having carried large blue and yellow Blue Circle nameplates. In 1984, the Lloyds and Scottish wagons were sold to Blue Circle and their number prefix was altered to BCC.

In addition to the Railease cement clinker hoppers mentioned in Chapter 2, Clyde Cement also operates a fleet of 88 t glw bogie Presflos. Built by Standard Wagon, using the same underframe design as that on the 'PBAs', these wagons normally run as a block-train between Clitheroe and Coatbridge as well as in Speedlink services to depots in Aberdeen and Dundee.

Finally, Rugby Cement owns a single bogie Presflo, formerly allocated to international traffic, which was used for many years as a static silo in Ardwick Goods yard, Manchester. Fitted with Y25 bogies, this 102 t glw vehicle could hold $87\frac{1}{2}$ t and was painted in an overall orange livery without company symbols.

Chapter 4

Flat Wagons

In his famous report on 'The Reshaping of British Railways' published in 1963, Dr Beeching predicted that the future for rail-hauled merchandise freight lay in the development of a countrywide network of Liner Trains, envisaged to be in full operation by 1970. To this end, British Rail constructed a considerable fleet of Freightliner flats, the few privately-owned flat wagons being inevitably of a more specialized nature. However, since 1983 Freightliner has begun to move out of the short-haul domestic business, in order to concentrate on maritime container movement, and the number of privately-owned flats has steadily increased, a trend that looks set to continue well into the future.

Table 11: *Flat wagons, two-axle*

Type	Number series		TOPS code	Builder	Date	Owner/Operator
Zinc block	BRT	95051–95074	PFA	Powell Duffryn	1968	BRTE/Commonwealth Smelting
Conflat	BRT	92600–92609	PFA	Procor	1985	BRTE/Cobra Railfreight
Conflat	PR	92690–92702	PFA	Procor	1986	Procor/Cobra Railfreight
Conflat	PR	93200–93240	PFA	Procor	1986–7	Procor/Kelly
Conflat	CAWD	92703–92864	PFA	Standard Wagon	1986–7	Cawoods
Conflat	F	93000	PFA	BREL Shildon	1981	Freightliners Ltd
Conflat	23 70 4424 001–005		PIA	EWAA	1984	STS/British Rail
Skip-carrier	BNFL	91000–91029	PFA	BREL Various	1978–9	British Nuclear Fuels

Zinc block wagons

The oldest two-axle flat wagons to survive on to TOPS were 24 zinc block vehicles hired to Commonwealth Smelting, Avonmouth. These 46 t glw wagons were 28 ft 2 in long, with Double-link suspension, a 15 ft wheelbase, and carried a 35 t load of zinc ingots. Very low sides were fitted, the ingots resting on low wooden battens fixed to the floor. By 1984, all 24 had been withdrawn, although BRT 95063 and BRT 95057 were subsequently converted to container flats and renumbered BRT 92600 and BRT 92601 respectively.

Container flat wagons, two-axle

The remaining BRTE two-axle container flats, BRT 92603–92609, and the Procor series, PR 92690–92702, are also rebuilds using 15 ft wheelbase underframes taken from redundant BRTE 46 t Class B tank

Above *BRT 92600, a 29½ t capacity conflat, was rebuilt from a zinc block wagon in 1985. The wagon livery is black with white lettering, while the potash container is a rusty lime green with yellow lettering. Tees Yard, September 1987.*

Below *Also recorded at Tees Yard in September 1987 was BRT 92605, a former 46 t tank wagon. Livery is again black with white lettering while the square container, used to carry rock salt, is in green, also with white lettering.*

The last 54 Cawoods coal container flats are fitted with metal plates at headstock height to protect the drawgear from spilled coal. CAWD 92862, one of this final batch, was photographed at Heywood in October 1987 when brand new. Livery is black with white lettering.

wagons. Apart from the removal of the tank, the conversion work involved re-springing, and the addition of container fixing points to allow the carriage of a single 20 ft container. Carrying capacity is $35\frac{1}{2}$ t for the ex-tank wagons, and $29\frac{1}{2}$ t for the former 'zinc blocks', all being hired to Cobra Railfreight to carry potash and rock salt from Boulby, as well as scrap metal to South Wales.

The second batch of Procor-owned two-axle conflats, PR 93201–93240, are purpose-built wagons designed to carry a 20 ft open-top container loaded with domestic coal. Leased to the Kelly Group, they were introduced in 1987 to replace out-dated railway-owned coal trucks, and they operate services from various Welsh collieries to Swansea Docks, where the containers are transhipped *en route* for Ireland.

As the anthracite is a particularly friable fossil fuel, containerization of this traffic had long been considered desirable so as to minimize handling and hence reduce the risk of degrading the product. Following extensive trials with the unique prototype wagon, PR 93200, the full operation finally commenced during the autumn of 1987.

Unlike the prototype, which had an unusually narrow floor, the remainder of this batch are fitted with conventional solebars, mounted below the top of the headstock so as to accommodate the increasingly popular 8 ft 6 in high containers, while the underframe is fitted with FAT 26 Double-link suspension to carry a $25\frac{1}{2}$ t payload.

Cawoods Container Services own a much larger fleet of dropped-floor two-axle conflats which are also used to carry containers of domestic coal destined for Ireland. Built by Standard Wagon, they differ from the Procor design in having a 16 ft 5 in wheelbase and long-link suspension. They can carry 36 t and run in block-train formations from South Wales and the North-east to Cawood's own private container terminal situated along the Manchester Ship Canal at Ellesmere Port, Cheshire.

Freightliners Ltd though a subsidiary of British Rail, is now treated as a private operator, hence the inclusion of their prototype skeletal container flat, F 93000, developed in collaboration with BREL to match the increasingly popular 40 ft long ISO containers that predominate on many deep-sea traffic flows. The wagon is 43 ft 2 in long, with FAT 7 Long-link suspension and a 29 ft $2\frac{1}{4}$ in wheelbase suitable for running at 75 mph. Unlike previous stock operated by Freightliner, F 93000 carries conventional buffers and drawgear at both ends, while the expensive disc brakes have given way to the cheaper clasp. The skeletal design of the wagon results in an impressive 30 t payload for an all-up weight of only 41 t. Since 1981, this prototype has undergone extensive evaluation in service and looks likely to become the forerunner of a fleet of similar vehicles expected to be ordered to replace the life-expired railway-owned bogie Freightliner flats. The livery of F 93000 is standard rail blue with white lettering.

The only ferry-fitted container flats registered in Britain are a small batch of $27\frac{1}{2}$ t wagons built in 1984 by Etabl Willynck Aubigny Aubec for STS. They have eight container fixing-points along each side making them suitable for standard ISO boxes, although they were originally built for a specialist traffic in demountable tank containers which unfortunately never materialized. All five wagons remained in store until 1987 when they were hired to British Rail to carry sugar beet loaded in 40 ft containers.

Skip-carrying wagons

British Nuclear Fuel's two-axle flat wagons are all former British Rail 31 t open 'OBAs', built at BREL's Shildon and Ashford works in the late 1970s. In 1983, 30 were rebuilt at Shildon and sold to BNFL to convey low-level radioactive waste in skips from its main site at Sellafield to a dump at Drigg, four miles away along the Cumbrian coast. The conversion entailed the removal of the original sides and the addition of movable, skip-locating brackets to the wagon floor. All the vehicles sold to BNFL were either built with FAT 24 taperleaf suspension, or else so modified before sale, though the maroon livery, with black underframe and white lettering, remained unchanged.

Container flat wagons, bogie

Greater Manchester County Council opened the first of four rail-connected Refuse Treatment Plants in 1981, at the start of a programme that would eventually encompass the entire area. Unlike the Greater London Council, which had introduced a similar rail-hauled waste disposal scheme some four years earlier, Greater Manchester decided to purchase its own fleet of bogie container flats rather than hire wagons from British Rail.

An initial batch of ten 80 t glw vehicles, built by the French company Remafer, were introduced on a block-train working between Dean Lane Treatment Plant and the disposal site at Appley Bridge, near Wigan, and as the three other treatment plants at Northenden, Salford, and Bredbury were brought on stream, a further two

The Remafer-built Greater Manchester bogie conflats have been fitted with modified buffers as can be seen in this view of GMC 92503, recorded at Manchester Victoria in April 1985. The livery of the wagon is black with white lettering while the container is painted orange and white with black lettering. Upon the creation of the Greater Manchester Waste Disposal Authority in 1986, the containers were relettered 'GMWDA', but there appears to be no intention to alter the wagon prefix letters.

Table 12: *Flat wagons, bogie*

Type	Number series		TOPS code	Builder	Date	Owner/Operator
Conflat	GMC	92500–92542	PFA	Various	1980–85	Greater Manchester Council
Conflat	GMC	92580–92588	PFA	Standard Wagon	1986	Greater Manchester Council
Conflat	AVON	92563–92579	PFA	Powell Duffryn	1985	Avon County Council
Conflat	RLS	92543–92562	PFA	Standard Wagon	1985	Railease/various
Conflat	RLS	92610–92651	PFA	Standard Wagon	1986	Railease/various
Conflat	RLS	95470–95486	PFA	Standard Wagon	1983	Railease/Cobra Railfreight
Conflat	RLS	92953–92963	PFA	Powell Duffryn	1987	Railease/BSC South Wales
Conflat	TIPH	93242–93489	PFA	Various	1987–8	Tiphook Rail
Warwell	MODA	95500–95583	PFV	Various	1942–44	Ministry of Defence, Army
Warflat	MODA	95105–95230	PFV	Metro Cammell	1940–42	Ministry of Defence, Army
Tankflat	MODA	95231–95232	PFX	Gloucester RC&W	1965	Ministry of Defence, Army
Warflat	MODA	95233–95297	PFB	BREL Shildon	1976–81	Ministry of Defence, Army
Flat	TWT	95450–95461	PFA	Procor	1977	Tyne & Wear Transport
Flatrol	NRMY	95400	PFO	BREL Derby	1949	National Railway Museum, York
Prologie	PR	95300	PFA	Procor	1985	Procor

batches of bogie flats were purchased, both from Standard Wagon. These differ from the Remafers in having only single-pipe air brakes, standard-height buffers and a more substantial solebar, although the larger batch, GMC 92510–92542, retain the Sambre-et-Meuse type bogies found on the earlier vehicles. GMC 92580–92588, on the other hand, have Gloucester GPS bogies, though all the Standard-built vehicles can run at 75 mph. In 1984, GMC 92500–92509, which had been delivered with low-height buffers, were modified to make them compatible with the rest, though they remain restricted to 60 mph. All can carry three purpose-built 20 ft refuse containers.

When Avon County Council introduced a similar rail-hauled waste disposal operation in 1986, it also chose to purchase its own wagons. Built by Powell Duffryn, they are similar to the later Greater Manchester flats, and run in block-train formation from the Bristol area to a disposal site at Calvert, Bucks. The wagons are painted black with white lettering; the containers are blue with black lettering.

Two further batches of conventional container flats were built by Standard Wagon in 1985. Both are owned by Railease, and at 67 ft 5¼ in over the headstocks, are 3 ft 8¼ in longer than the GMC wagons, although they retain Sambre-et-Meuse bogies centred at 46 ft. Capacity is also increased by two tonnes to 62 t, both batches having fixing-points to accommodate all standard-size containers. Until 1986, RLS 92543–92562 were leased to Ciba Geigy, for resin and plastics traffic to Ireland via Stranraer and Fishguard, but in that year

RLS 92546, one of the 82 t Railease bogie conflats operated by Ciba–Geigy. Each of the three 20 ft curtain-sided containers contains a plastic tank which carries amino-resins. The containers are blue and the wagon black with white lettering. Heywood, October 1987.

Above *Railease also owns the bogie conflats operated by Pedigree Petfood. Illustrated at Ardwick in October 1986 is RLS 92617, loaded with two purpose-built 30 ft curtain-sided containers which carry a chocolate brown livery with yellow lettering. Both types of curtain-sided containers are designed for unloading by top-lift fork-lift trucks.*

Below *After spending a year in trial service with Freightliners Ltd, the bulk of the final batch of Railease bogie conflats, RLS 92636–92651, were converted into drop-side open wagons for Redland roof tiles. RLS 92642 is seen outside the workshop at Heywood having been fitted with a second floor at headstock height, raised ends, six drop-doors per side and numerous load restraining straps. The new bodywork is painted light green with 'Redland' in red and other lettering black.*

RLS 92551-92562 were fitted with semi-permanent coil cradles and hired to Isis Link for steel coil traffic from Ravenscraig. In 1988, RLS 92545 and RLS 92546 were sold to Redland Aggregates after being fitted with boom conveyers so as to act as 'Transfer Wagons' with the 'Self Discharging Hopper Train' (see Chapter 5). The first 22 wagons from the second batch, RLS 92610-92631, are leased to Pedigree Petfood, and carry two 30 ft curtain-sided containers in block-trains from Melton Mowbray, while the rest are hired to Freightliners Ltd.

Railease's remaining bogie flats comprise two specialist types. RLS 95470-95486 are leased to Cobra Railfreight and operate between Boulby and the ICI fertilizer plant at Severn Beach, loaded with two purpose-built containers each holding 20 t of potash. These wagons are fitted with detachable bolsters since the Cobra containers are of two different lengths, while their complete removal transforms the vehicles into standard conflats suitable for carrying two 20 ft ISO containers.

Even more specialized are RLS 92953-92963, having been built from redundant bogie tank underframes. Only the two end sections of the tank underframe, complete with bogies, buffers, and headstocks, have been re-used, producing a vehicle 47 ft 1 in long with a 76 t capacity. All 11 wagons are hired to British Steel and can normally be found working between Llanwern steelworks and the tinplate works at Ebbw Vale, loaded with cold-reduced steel coil. The coils are carried in specially-designed hooded containers to protect them from rust, two containers to a wagon.

Tiphook Rail, a subsidiary of the Tiphook container rental company, introduced its first bogie container flats in 1987. While of conventional design, the

---

REDA 92545, one of the two former Railease conflats sold to Redland and recoded PXA. Both are fitted with adjustable conveyors to assist in unloading the Redland 'Self-Discharge Hopper Train'. Livery is pale green with black lettering and bogies. Heywood, April 1988.

The detachable bolsters fitted to Railease bogie container flat RLS 95481 are clearly evident in this view taken at Heywood in December 1987. These wagons carry the 'Cobra' livery of lime green with yellow lettering and black bogies.

RLS 92958, one of 11 container flats built from redundant bogie tank underflames, suitably shortened, was photographed awaiting repair at Heywood in October 1987 well away from its usual haunts. The dropped ends of the solebars give these wagons a distinctive appearance. Livery is black with white lettering; the containers, both of which would be hooded when in service, are blue with white markings.

The first of the Tiphook 90 t container flats, TIPH 93242, recorded at Ardwick, January 1988. Livery is overall blue with white lettering; the two unusual steel containers are pale grey with no other markings other than the blue and orange 'Tiphook' logo.

skeletal floors are built by Rautaruuki of Finland, the Gloucester GPS bogies and brake gear being added after their arrival in Britain. Unlike the remainder of the Tiphook rail fleet, these 82 t bogie conflats do not carry 12-digit ferry numbers, because the Gloucester bogie is not UIC approved. Intended for various traffics, initial indications suggested that this would include use on the Spillers petfood service between Glasgow and Wisbech, while the batch TIPH 93282–93289, which was built by Powell Duffryn from bogie tank underframes, carries steel coil in curtain-sided containers.

Warwells and Warflats

The Ministry of Defence owns a large number of bogie flat wagons, used to transport military equipment between various depots throughout the country. During the Second World War, all of the 'Big Four' railway companies shared in the construction of a 77 t glw 'Warwell' design for the army. This featured a heavily constructed wagon body with a floor which sloped down between the bogies to form a well capable of accommodating small tanks and other military vehicles. All were 43 ft long, with diamond-frame, primary suspension bogies at 33 ft centres, vacuum brakes and carrying 51 t when the load was positioned centrally. Screw-jacks were fitted beneath each buffer, which could be screwed down to rail height for stability when end loading. Since 1976, some 32 'Warwells' have been refurbished with Gloucester GPS bogies and air-brakes, the remaining 53 vacuum-braked wagons being withdrawn in 1981.

Also built during the Second World War was the first batch of 'Warflats'. These 71 t glw vehicles had wooden floors, supported by distinctive 'fish-belly' type solebars, and could also carry 51 t. At 40 ft over the

Although designed to carry military vehicles, the MoD's fleet of bogie wagons can often be seen with other loads. MODA 95511, a refurbished 'Warwell', is seen at Wellington, Shropshire, in October 1986 loaded with a communication centre. The livery is standard Army olive green bodywork with yellow lettering, with black bogies and underframe gear.

MODA 95237, a 71 t glw 'Warflat' built at Shildon in 1976, is seen at Blackburn in May 1987. Note the screw-jacks at the end of the vehicle, the deep, straight-channel solebars and the TOPS number painted on the head-stock. The livery is standard olive green, including the bogies, with yellow lettering.

headstocks, they were shorter than the 'Warwells', with secondary coil suspension bogies centred at 30 ft. A handful survived in store until 1987.

The two 'Tankflats', built in 1965, were similar in appearance to the early 'Warflats'. However, they were some 2 ft shorter, were fitted with dual brakes and could carry 54 t if positioned centrally. Both had been withdrawn by 1982.

To replace the vacuum-braked 'Warflats' and the 'Tankflats', a larger air-braked design was put into construction at BREL's Shildon works from 1976 onwards. These 71 t glw wagons are 42 ft 6 in long with a wooden floor supported by straight channel solebars, and are fitted with Gloucester GPS bogies centred at 31 ft. As such they

can be accommodated at most MoD installations, some of which feature tightly-curved sidings. A 50 t payload can be carried, and the integral headstock-mounted screw-jacks allow bogie removal in the field so that in an emergency a wagon can be adapted into a loading ramp. All the MoD Army fleet are painted olive green with yellow or white lettering, some of the earlier types having black bogies.

Miscellaneous flat wagons, bogie

Twelve new bogie flat wagons were purchased by Tyne & Wear Transport from Procor in 1977, initially for use in the construction phase, and subsequently for maintenance, of the Tyne & Wear Metro

TWT 95457 was the only one of the dozen Tyne and Wear bogie flats to remain in its original condition when photographed at North Shields in August 1987. The basic livery is overall black with white lettering; at each end of the solebar are yellow patches with the Metro symbol in blue and black and the wagon's fleet number.

One of two flats fitted with Geismar Rail Loading Arms, TWT 95459, awaits its introduction into traffic at North Shields in August 1987. The arms are painted yellow with black markings.

Two of the Tyne & Wear flat wagons are fitted with ends and drop-sides, including TWT 95455, seen at North Shields in August 1987. Livery of the bodywork is dark grey.

system. All are air-braked, 62 ft 4 in long, with second-hand Gloucester cast steel bogies centred at 46 ft 11 in and can carry 50 t. Most have had semi–permanent structures built on to them, including three with scaffolding for overhead line maintenance; two with Geismar rail loading arms; two with dropsides; two with cable drum carriers; and two with small cranes. All twelve are painted black with white lettering; the Metro symbol in blue and black is applied on a yellow patch at one end of the solebar. Although passed for running on British Rail metals, it is rare for any of this fleet to leave the Metro system.

NRMY 95400, owned by the National Railway Museum, is a former British Railway Flatrol MHH, now in use to move exhibits around the exhibition site at York. Originally numbered B 900402, this wagon was built in 1949 to diagram 2/511 and can carry 41 t. It is 58 ft long with secondary coil suspension bogies centred at 48 ft and is normally confined to the museum sidings, although it did participate in 'Rocket 150', the 1980 celebration of the 150th anniversary of the Rainhill Trials, loaded with the Welshpool & Llanfair Light Railway's

TWT 95453 has been fitted with various cable drums in addition to an Atlas Crane and operates as part of the Overhead Line Maintenance Train, in company with the OHL Scaffolding wagons, which can be seen in the background of this view taken at South Gosforth in August 1987.

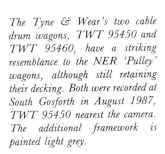

The Tyne & Wear's two cable drum wagons, TWT 95450 and TWT 95460, have a striking resemblance to the NER 'Pulley' wagons, although still retaining their decking. Both were recorded at South Gosforth in August 1987, TWT 95450 nearest the camera. The additional framework is painted light grey.

The 'Prologie', PR 95300, has spent much of its life in store at Swansea, where it was photographed in August 1986 when temporarily carrying a Shell LPG tank underframe. The unusual design necessitated situating the brake cylinders on top of the headstocks. Livery is overall blue with white lettering on black patches (P. Bartlett).

narrow-gauge locomotive *The Earl.*

The 'Prologie' wagon, PR 95300, is an interesting attempt at contriving a 'piggy-back' vehicle that would have a useful purpose within the restricted British loading gauge. The design was developed by Procor in co-operation with British Rail's Research Division and the West German wagon builders Talbot, the prototype entering trial service in 1985. The main features of the vehicle are a long, flat-bedded well, slung very low between the two specially constructed inside-frame bogies, and the bogies themselves, which are fitted with small-diameter wheels. This produces a low–deck wagon capable of carrying road vehicles up to 38 t, as well as the 9 ft 6 in containers now finding favour in many traffics, without any of the length constraints inherent with previous well-

wagon designs. Unfortunately, the initial trials failed to satisfy British Rail's running requirements, due to guidance problems encountered with the small-wheel bogies, and the wagon was withdrawn in 1986 pending further modifications.

Tiphook Rail has also developed a 'piggy-back' wagon to run within the British loading gauge. The key feature of this vehicle is the deck, designed to pivot at one end, the other end of which can be swung laterally to one side of the wagon giving access for a road trailer to be driven on. With the trailer in position, the deck is then swung back into place and locked and the wagon is then ready to proceed. Construction of the prototype two-axle wagon was completed in Finland in 1988 with extensive trials anticipated before the type enters service.

Chapter 5

Open Hopper Wagons

While a number of covered hopper designs date from before the Second World War, the emergence of the privately-owned open hopper is a more recent phenomenon, resulting largely from the building boom of the 1970s. A number of large fleets have now been built and the type has become one of the most common on British Rail.

Salt hoppers, two-axle

In 1971, Standard Wagon introduced the first fleet of bulk salt hoppers, initially for hire to BP Chemicals. The shape of these 46 t glw wagons was most distinctive, featuring a steeply-angled body and an unusually long 26 ft 7 in underframe, with a 16 ft wheelbase. Four small vertical ribs sup-

Table 13: *Open hopper wagons, two-axle*

Type	Number series		TOPS code	Builder	Date	Owner/Operator
Salt	PR	8201–8255	PGA	Standard Wagon	1971	Procor/various
Salt	PR	8256–8300	PGA	Charles Roberts	1974	Procor/various
Salt	PR	8901–8918	PGA	Charles Roberts	1974	Procor/various
Aggregate	AR	14201–14264	PGA	Charles Roberts	1972–4	Amey Roadstone
Aggregate	PR	14000–14151	PGA	Various	1972	Procor/Foster Yeoman
Aggregate	PR	14688–14704	PGA	Standard Wagon	1972	Procor/Amey Roadstone
Aggregate	PR	14706–14749	PGA	Procor	1978	Procor/Amey Roadstone
Aggregate	PR	14176–14197	PGA	Procor	1979	Procor/Foster Yeoman
Aggregate	PR	14265–14388	PGA	Procor	1979–80	Procor/various
Aggregate	PR	14434–14466	PGA	Procor	1981	Procor/Foster Yeoman
Aggregate	BRT	14600–14654	PGA	Standard Wagon	1974	BRTE/various
Aggregate	TAMC	14655–14687	PGA	Standard Wagon	1974	Tarmac Roadstone
Aggregate	TAMC	14840–14870	PGA	Procor	1979	Tarmac Roadstone
Aggregate	TAMC	14900–14921	PGA	Standard Wagon	1979	Tarmac Roadstone
Aggregate	RLS	14705	PGA	Standard Wagon	1977	Railease/Tarmac Roadstone
Aggregate	TBR	14500–14522	PGA	Procor	1980	Tilbury Roadstone
Aggregate	REDA	14750–14839	PGA	Various	1978–84	Redland Aggregates
Aggregate	TCS	14400–14432	PGA	BREL Shildon	1973	Tilling Construction
Gypsum	APCM	19551–19589	PGA	BREL Shildon	1970	Assoc Portland Cement
Limestone	BSTE	18000–18114	PGA	Standard Wagon	1975	British Steel, Teesside
Minerals	SRW	18500–18529	PGA	Standard Wagon	1982	Standard Wagon/various
Demonstrator	DAVS	14433	PGA	W.H. Davis	1976	W.H. Davis & Sons
Demonstrator	DAVS	19999	PGO	W.H. Davis	1981	W.H. Davis & Sons
Self-discharge	REDA	16000–16203(r)	PGA	Standard Wagon	1988	Redland Aggregates

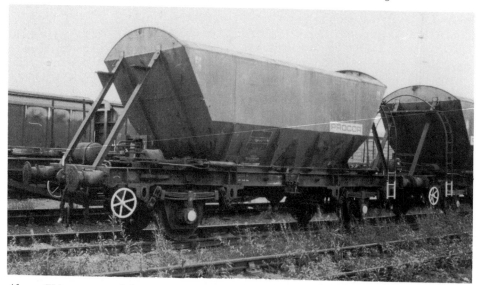

Above *This re-sprung salt hopper PR 8230 was recorded at Tees Yard in September 1987. Livery is rusty yellow with the 'Procor' symbol in blue and white, white lettering on black patches and black underframe.*

Below *The end-ladder design, deep, flat-sided solebar and tarpaulin cover are all evident in this view of PR 8296, taken at Warrington in July 1987. The wagon had recently been repainted with grey body, white lettering and black underframe, but it was unlikely to remain in this condition for long given the abrasive and staining nature of its load of salt.*

ported the sloping part of the sides with two larger supports at each end which also carried the sharply-curved ladders and small inspection platform. The original FAT 4 UIC suspension was subsequently replaced by various types in order to permit 60 mph operation, while two wagons were experimentally built with shorter bodies. In 1980, a number received hood supports for use in aluminium oxide traffic between Hull and Stafford, but by 1987 all the survivors were carrying salt from the Cleveland potash mine at Boulby.

The second fleet of salt hoppers, built by Charles Roberts, was a 51 t glw design which quickly displaced the earlier vehicles from the BP traffic between Cheshire and South Wales. Wagons of this type occupy two separate blocks in the number series but are otherwise identical, and, though only 24 ft 9 in long, carry over 37 t. The large hopper body is strengthened by five vertical ribs on each side which extend from the solebar to the top of the side, while footsteps at each corner give access to short ladders mounted longitudinally on the end. These in turn lead to an inspection platform running across the full width of the end which also provides additional support for the hopper body. To protect the salt from weather contamination, five metal hoops can be fixed across the top to support a tarpaulin cover. Two sets of mechanically-operated hopper doors are located between the wheels, the operating handle and ratchet mechanism being located in the centre of the unusually deep, flat-sided solebar, which slopes down at each end to a conventional headstock. BSC Friction Pedestal suspension at an 18 ft 2 in wheelbase was fitted from new. Wagons still carrying salt have been hired to ICI since 1981, but a reduction in this traffic has seen a growing number reallocated to the movement of aggregates.

Aggregate hoppers, two-axle

The 51 t salt hoppers were a variant of an existing design which had been introduced some two years previously for aggregates traffic. The building boom of the 1970s saw the construction industry having to look to remote quarries to satisfy the huge demand for crushed stone, particularly in the South-east, and only rail could provide the bulk transport required. As part of the long-term contracts signed at that time, British Rail insisted on the provision of company-owned, or leased, modern air-braked wagons for any substantial movements, and though demand has since slackened, the advantages of rail transport have seen many companies continuing to invest in their own wagon fleets.

Most two-axle hoppers derive from the initial Charles Roberts design, built in 1972 for hire to Foster Yeoman. These vehicles have part-sloping sides and ends supported by small ribs, with the deep, flat-sided solebars and ladder arrangement as on the salts. After a few years in service, they were fitted with shaped metal plates, fixed beneath the inspection platforms, to protect the brake cylinders from damage when being loaded with stone. PR 14025–14095 were built by Standard Wagon, the major difference being the locating of the brake cylinders beneath the headstocks, obviating the need for protective plates. Unlike Foster Yeoman, Amey Roadstone, another major quarrying company, initially chose to purchase its own wagons, but, after a batch of 64 vehicles had been acquired, it also decided to lease, and indeed in 1986 the original batch were sold back to Procor for re-hire to Amey Roadstone.

Further construction of this design commenced in 1978, some four more batches being built by Procor up to 1981. Major modifications involved the use of straight-channel solebars, with Gloucester Floating-

BRT 14611 is one of the 51 t aggregate hoppers leased to Peakstone of Buxton. Note the straight-channel solebar, preferred by the builders Standard Wagon, and the attractive livery which comprises mustard body and underframe, with black 'Peakstone' lettering and symbol, 'BRT' symbol in red, black and white, and other lettering white, some on black patches.

axle suspension from PR 14320, although the 16 ft wheelbase was retained. The body shape was slightly altered and strengthened by 'T'-angle struts, while conventional side-mounted ladders were fitted, capacity remaining at some 38 t.

In 1982, PR 14329 was the subject of an interesting experiment, its standard hopper body being replaced by a prototype self-discharging type divided internally into two compartments, the floor of each being formed by separate, externally powered, conveyor belts. The load was discharged through a single central opening in the underframe, but various trials proved unsuccessful and the idea was abandoned.

Foster Yeoman's fleet is painted light grey with black lettering, solebars and underframe, the first batch originally having dark grey solebars. The company name is usually carried in white on a blue panel along the flat part of the side, and the wagons operate from the company's quarry

at Merehead, near Cranmore, to various distribution depots in the South and South-east. Initially, the Amey Roadstone vehicles were yellow with black solebars and underframe, but in 1983 they were re-painted pale mustard with grey solebars and underframe, the 'ARC' initials being picked out in grey with all other lettering in white. These wagons operate from quarries at Whatley, near Frome, and Tytherington, near Bristol, to depots in the Midlands and the South.

Following the success of these initial operations, a number of other companies decided to invest in their own wagon fleets. In the North-west, the Staveley Lime Company introduced block-train workings from its quarry at Dove Holes, near Buxton, to depots in Salford and Liverpool, using 27 hoppers, BRT 14600–14626, which were hired from BRTE. The remainder of this batch were initially hired to Amey Roadstone and more recently have seen use

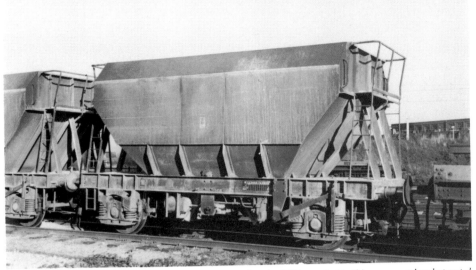

TAMC 14905 is another 51 t aggregate hopper built by Standard Wagon, but in this case owned and operated by Tarmac Roadstone. These vehicles, which have a more 'chunky' appearance than earlier hoppers, normally run in block-train formations, although this example was recorded at Warrington in August 1987 when en route to works for routine maintenance.

carrying rock salt from Boulby.

Tarmac Roadstone also owns quarries in the Buxton area, its first batch of Standard-built hoppers being originally allocated to workings from Topley Pike to depots in Widnes and Salford. Built in 1974 with deep, flat-sided solebars, these wagons carried an attractive brown and white livery and were eventually transferred to Cliffe Hill quarry, Leicestershire, in 1979. Their replacements at Topley Pike were also built by Standard Wagon, but TAMC 14900–14921 were to a completely new design. The hopper ends have a more pronounced slope while the side slope is considerably reduced, with conventional side-mounted ladders providing access to a small inspection platform. Length is only 21 ft 7 in with a 15 ft wheelbase, though capacity remains at over 38 t, the underframe being fitted with straight-channel solebars and pneumatically-operated hopper doors. RLS 14705, the prototype for this design,

also operates out of Topley Pike, its major differences being a single set of hopper doors and a more primitive ladder arrangement. This batch carries a yellow livery, but for its third fleet, also built in 1979, Tarmac returned to the brown and white colour scheme previously used in 1974. This final batch follow Procor's standard design for the late 1970s with straight-channel solebars and conventional side-mounted ladders, the majority running from Frome to depots in the South-east.

The Tilbury Roadstone fleet is also to the same basic design, though somewhat higher with a pronounced slope to the sides and a deeper lip along the top. There is also a noticeable skirt between the lower part of the hopper and the solebar, but the underframe is identical with Gloucester suspension units. In 1986, this fleet was sold to Redland, the black 'Tilbury Roadstone' name being replaced by 'Redland' in red on the white panel which covers the flat part

REDA 16200, a 'Self-Discharge Hopper Train' 'outer' wagon. Note the conveyor belt which is extended beyond the headstock when unloading. This train is particularly suitable for short-term traffic flows as it can be unloaded without the need for any on-site facilities other than a rail siding. Body and solebars are pale green; the 'Redland' name is red, while other lettering and suspension units are black. Heywood, April 1988.

of the side. The remainder of the body is red, and the solebars and underframe are black; these wagons operate to various depots in East Anglia.

Redland has also purchased a large fleet of its own, the bulk being constructed between 1978 and 1980 by Standard Wagon to a design that combines the standard 22 ft 3 in long, 16 ft wheelbase underframe with a hopper body similar to that fitted to the Tarmac hoppers, TAMC 149xx. In 1986, a number were fitted with pneumatic doors operated via the train's air brake reservoir pipe in order to speed discharge. REDA 14781–14786 were built by Procor in 1984 to the same design as the final batch of Tarmac's, and all operate from Redland's quarry at Mountsorrel to depots in the London area and in East Anglia. The initial

body livery of white with red and blue stripes has been gradually replaced by pale green with red lettering; solebars and underframes remain black. In 1988, Redland introduced its revolutionary 'Self Discharge Hopper Train'. Built by Standard Wagon, each of the four prototype trains comprises ten 51 t glw two-axle hoppers, semi-permanently coupled, and fitted with a continuous conveyor belt at solebar level on to which the hoppers discharge.

Only one batch of modern aggregate hoppers has been built by BREL, the 33 51 t glw Tilcon hoppers which operate from Tilling Construction's quarry at Rylstone, near Skipton, to depots in Hull and Leeds. They are higher than other aggregate hoppers, with steeply-angled sides and ends, the sides being supported by five angled buttresses and the ends by protective plates fitted over the brake cylinders. Their clamshell-type hopper doors are pneumatically-operated and the 22 ft 8 in long underframe carries BSC Friction Pedestal suspension. The hopper body is painted Wedgwood blue with the word Tilcon picked out in white on a maroon panel, and the double 'T' motif in white on a black panel. Solebars are maroon, with the suspension units and brake gear black.

Other open hoppers, two-axle

In addition to the Tilcon hoppers, BREL's Shildon works also built a batch of 46 t glw hoppers for carrying gypsum, a mineral used in the manufacture of certain types of cement. Introduced in 1970, they are a smaller version of the familiar railway-owned 'Merry-go-Round' coal hopper, but are only 29 ft long, with two sets of hopper doors fitted with automatic discharge gear to allow for unloading on the move. As gypsum is a much denser commodity than coal, capacity is still 33 t, and the wagons normally run between the British Gypsum mine at Mountfield, Sussex, and the Blue Circle Cement factory in Northfleet, Kent.

Also fitted with automatic discharge gear are the large fleet of limestone hoppers owned by British Steel, Teesside. Built in 1975, they serve the massive steelworks complex at Redcar and, unlike other wagons of this type, are fitted with BSC primary coil suspension set on a 16 ft 6 in wheelbase. The body design is also unusual in having a very high lip along the top of the sides and ends and no inspection platforms. Capacity is 37 t, the fleet normally running in block-train formations between Redmire and Redcar. When, in 1982, a number of this fleet became redundant, they were resold to Standard Wagon and renumbered in the SRW 185xx series after having been modified for general mineral

APCM 19557, a gypsum hopper, recorded when stopped for repair at Hoo Junction in April 1980. The bodywork is galvanized steel with black lettering and underframe. The central panel is picked out in yellow with a blue circle (R. Silsbury).

As detailed in the text, a number of the British Steel Teesside hoppers have been rebuilt for general aggregate traffic. One such vehicle, SRW 18509, was recorded at Warrington in September 1987 sparkling in its new overall white livery with 'Railease' in blue and other lettering in white on black patches.

The automatic door-operating mechanism can be clearly seen in this view of BSTE 18058, taken at Tees Yard in September 1987. Note the lack of prefix letters on the vehicle's data panel, a feature common to this fleet. Originally painted a pale green, these wagons were being repainted in the grey and black livery illustrated here, with blue and white British Steel symbol.

traffic by the fitting of inspection platforms, modified door gear and cut-down sides. Subsequently, the majority of the modified vehicles were hired by British Rail to carry sand from Holmethorpe, near Redhill, to Crosfield's chemical plant in Warrington.

Finally, mention must be made of the two wagons built by W.H. Davis of Shirebrook as speculative ventures in the hopes of attracting future orders. DAVS 14433 was a conventional 51 t glw, 38 t capacity aggregate hopper fitted with Gloucester Floating-axle suspension and most of the features common to this type. It initially appeared in a green and yellow livery before being repainted red with black lettering. The second vehicle, DAVS 19999, was a 36 t glw, $27\frac{1}{2}$ t capacity sand hopper, built on a redundant 16 ft wheelbase underframe taken from an ex–pallet van. Both wagons appeared at various exhibitions and open days but were never used in traffic and had been withdrawn by 1987.

The unique 51 t aggregate hopper built by W.H. Davis, DAVS 14433, photographed when stored out of use at Shirebrook in November 1985. By this date it was painted red with black 'Davis' symbol and underframe.

Table 14: *Open hopper wagons, bogie*

Type	Number series	TOPS code	Builder	Date	Owner/Operator
Limestone	ICIM 19000–19164	PHV	Charles Roberts	1936–58	ICI Mond
Iron ore	BSSH 13060–13182	PHO	Charles Roberts	1952–8	British Steel, Shotton
Ballast	GLE 15000–15005	PHO	Metropolitan C & W	1928–36	Grant, Lyon & Eagre
Ballast	TWT 15100–15102	PHA	Metropolitan C & W	1936	Tyne & Wear Transport
Aggregate	MPHY 17701–17712	PHA	Charles Roberts	1968–9	Murphy Aggregates
Aggregate	MAR 17713–17722	PHA	W.H. Davis	1983	Marcon
Aggregates	ELC 17501–17520	PHA	Charles Roberts	1970	Equipment Leasing/Brett
Aggregates	BHQ 17101–17121	PHA	W.H. Davis	1986	Bardon Hill Quarries
Aggregates	RHR 17301–17327	PHA	W.H. Davis	1987	RH Roadstone
Aggregates	HALL 13700–13712	PHA	Standard Wagon	1984	Hall Aggregates
Aggregates	RMC 17201–17224	PHA	Standard Wagon	1986	Ready Mixed Concrete
Aggregates	PR 17801–17837	PHA	Procor	1984	Procor/Foster Yeoman
Aggregates	FR 17001–17011	PHA	Installation MC	1971–2	Francis Parker

Limestone, iron ore and ballast hoppers, bogie

ICI Mond's fleet of bogie limestone hoppers are amongst the oldest privately-owned wagons still in regular use on British Rail, a number having been built as early as 1936. Construction continued intermittently until 1953, all to the same design, with a 35 t capacity body divided into two compartments and supported by six

Above *ICIM 19129, one of the Charles Roberts-built limestone bogie hoppers, photographed at Northwich in August 1987. Apart from the addition of roller bearings, this wagon remains in virtually its original condition, although it has recently been repainted pale grey with the number panel in white on a black ground. Note the raised 'ICI' letters on the side; an earlier version of the livery had these painted orange.*

Below *TWT 15101, one of the rebuilt ex-Southern Railway 'Walrus' ballast hoppers, awaits loading at North Shields on the Tyne & Wear Metro in August 1987. This vehicle carries overall black livery with white lettering. The yellow patch near the top of the second panel should carry the blue and black 'Metro' symbol.*

substantial ribs along each side and two angled struts at each end. Gloucester plateback bogies, standard on the post-war build, have gradually been fitted to the entire fleet, replacing the diamond-frame bogies found under the earlier wagons. As they were intended to operate along the severely graded lines between Tunstead and Northwich, vacuum brakes were provided from new, the single brake cylinder being a prominent feature on one end. The original livery comprised pale green bodywork with white lettering, and black solebar and bogies.

In the 1950s, British Steel, Shotton, bought a number of similar, but unfitted, hoppers from Charles Roberts, to transport imported iron ore from Bidston Dock, Merseyside, to the steelworks at Shotton, near Wrexham. When steelmaking ceased there in 1983, ICI purchased the bulk of this fleet, some 13 being refurbished and vacuum-braked for future use in limestone traffic. They were repainted in the later ICI livery of light grey and renumbered ICIM 19152–19164.

Grant, Lyon & Eagre, a Scunthorpe-based civil engineering firm, owned six former Southern Railway 'Walrus' bogie ballast hoppers, purchased from British Rail in the 1960s for use on railway-related construction projects. All six were built by the Metropolitan Carriage & Wagon Company; GLE 15000–15002 were from the original 1928 batch, while GLE 15003–15005 were from the slightly modified batch built in 1936 to Southern Railway diagram 1774, rated at $61\frac{1}{2}$ rather than $60\frac{1}{2}$ t glw. All were unfitted, carried 40 t, and remained virtually in their original condition in private ownership, complete with diamond-frame bogies centred at 23 ft. All six were withdrawn in 1982 following completion of work on the Midland City Line electrification scheme

between Bedford and Moorgate. Livery was all-over black with white lettering.

Tyne & Wear Transport also own three ex-Southern Railway ballast hoppers from the 1936 batch. However, following purchase in 1977 they were air-braked and fitted with Gloucester FBT 5 bogies, before being despatched to Newcastle in 1978. To conform to axle-load restrictions on the Metro, they are rated at 50 t glw, 28 t capacity, and are fitted with raised mesh screens at each end in order to protect the operator from the overhead live wires when climbing up to check whether the hopper is fully discharged.

Aggregate hoppers, bogie

Murphy Aggregates introduced a dozen modern bogie hoppers in 1968 to carry sea-dredged gravel from their depot at Angerstein Wharf, on the Thames, to various terminals in the South-east. These 102 t glw wagons are 50 ft 7 in long, with Gloucester cast steel bogies centred at 37 ft 10 in, and carry 75 t. The specially-shaped body has a long, rectangular top opening and three sets of discharge doors situated towards the centre of the floor. The bogies are carried on short stub-frames to allow lorry-mounted conveyors to be driven underneath when unloading. A further batch of ten similar hoppers was built for Marcon in 1983, the main difference being the fitting of Gloucester GPS bogies and a nose cowling on the end to protect the brake gear. At the same time, the earlier wagons were transferred to Marcon (the ready-mixed concrete arm of Murphy Aggregates), and recoded 'MAR'. Since 1984, Marcon has shifted its entire operation to the Brett Aggregates depot at Cliffe in Kent.

Also operating from Cliffe with sea-dredged gravel is a fleet of 102 t glw hoppers owned by Equipment Leasing and hired to

Brett. While similar in design to the Murphy hoppers, they are only 41 ft 7 in long and present a more robust appearance. They have full length solebars, Gloucester Mk 4 cast steel bogies, and run as a block-train to terminals at Purley and Salfords in South London.

W.H. Davis, having built the Marcon hoppers in 1983, further developed this particular design with two batches of 90 t glw vehicles which appeared in 1986 and 1987 intended for stone traffic. The first batch, owned by Bardon Hill Quarries, are fitted with French Y25C bogies and carry 68½ t. They have full-length solebars with prominent end-plates to support the hopper body and protect the brake gear. Inspection ladders are fitted at diagonally opposite corners and they run as a block-train following a complicated programme which takes them to quarries at Westbury, Croft and Bardon Hill, as well as to stone terminals at

West Drayton, Theale and Brentford, in the course of a week.

The second batch, owned by R.H. Roadstone, a subsidiary of Tarmac, have Gloucester GPS bogies fitted to short stub-frames and four sets of discharge doors. The hopper body is similar to the Bardon Hill wagons and is finished in a greenish-grey livery with black lettering, solebar and running gear. Intended to carry limestone and sand, this fleet operates from loading terminals in Somerset and Essex to depots in the south of England.

Standard Wagon has built two batches of an 88 t glw 66 t capacity bogie hopper design for Ready Mixed Concrete. Both batches have a curved 'hog's-back'-shaped hopper body carried on French Y25C bogies centred at 31 ft 9½ in, the under-frames featuring flat-sided solebars, with inspection ladders and small brake gear protection plates at each end. All carry an

The distinctive shape of RMC 17218, an 88 t bogie hopper belonging to Ready Mixed Concrete, can be seen in this view, recorded at Peak Forest in May 1987. The bodywork is orange with a broad white panel along the top of each side, with black lettering and underframe.

orange and white livery, though there are detailed differences between the two batches. The first are lettered up for Hall Aggregates, an RMC subsidiary, and carry sea-dredged gravel from Newhaven to terminals at Tolworth and Crawley, while the second batch are based at the Dove Holes quarry, Peak Forest, and carry limestone to Washwood Heath and Salford, as well as the occasional load of granite from Penmaenmawr on the North Wales coast.

Procor's fleet of 102 t glw hoppers is unique in being constructed from wide extruded aluminium sections produced by Alusuisse to a design developed jointly with Procor and Foster Yeoman. The body shape is also unusual as its cladding slopes towards the headstocks, and the sides end in a strip which is higher than the headstocks. The four sets of discharge doors are prominent between the Gloucester GPS bogies which are centred at 37 ft 3¾ in, and the lightweight design allows a carrying capacity of over 81 t. In 1986, the Instanter couplings and buffers were removed from these wagons, being replaced by automatic buckeyes in order to allow the operation of longer, heavier trains. All 37 vehicles operated between Merehead quarry and the Foster Yeoman terminal at Theale in Berkshire. Body livery is unpainted aluminium, with the Yeoman symbol picked out in blue.

Another batch of unique vehicles are the 11 side-discharge hoppers owned by Francis Parker Limited, now part of the Tarmac group. These 91 t glw wagons were built by Installation Manufacturing Contractors of Hartlepool in 1971 and have 5 ft 11 in wheelbase bogies supplied by Franco Belge fitted at 24 ft 4 in centres, the overall length being 41 ft and the capacity 67 t. The

PR 17818, an aluminium-bodied bogie hopper built by Procor in 1974, was photographed when on display at the Eastleigh Open Day, October 1986. Bodywork is finished in natural alloy with the 'Yeoman' name and symbol in blue and white, other lettering white on black patches. Headstocks and solebars are blue while the bogies and discharge doors are black with white markings (P. Fidczuk).

The first of the bogie gravel hoppers, FR 17001, was recorded at Fratton in May 1979 when newly painted in yellow ochre livery with white lettering and black running gear. The wagon was returning to Chichester after a visit to Eastleigh for tyre turning (R. Silsbury).

lower half of the hopper sides comprise two top-hinged doors, the operating cranks for which are located on the wagon ends. This small fleet operates as a block-train on the short five-mile haul from gravel workings at Lavant to a processing terminal at Drayton, the use of rail being one of the planning conditions laid down owing to the inadequate road system around Chichester. Initial livery was grey with white lettering, with the name 'Francis' in green on a large white patch over the two centre fixed side-panels. In 1979 the wagons were repainted yellow ochre, a shade which blends well with the gravel stains, the lettering remaining white and the bogies black.

Chapter 6

Motor Vehicle Carrying Wagons

Automotive traffic on British Rail, comprising both the distribution of finished cars and the inter-factory movement of components, is an important part of the freight business and warrants its own status as a separate Railfreight sub-sector. Traditionally, the movement of components has been in railway-owned wagons, increasingly supplemented in recent years by continentally registered ferry vans, both types being outside the scope of this volume, but the majority of new vehicles are carried by the wide range of specialist, privately-owned wagons listed in Table 15.

Table 15: *Motor vehicle carrying wagons*

Type	Number series		TOPS code	Builder	Date	Owner/Operator
Cartic	MAT	90000–90399	PJB	Various	1966–72	MAT Transauto
Cartic	SILC	90420–90543	PJB	Rootes Pressing	1966	Silcock & Colling
Cartic	PR	90800–90871	PJB	Various	1969–72	Procor/Toleman
Procor 80	PR	90872–90907	PLA	Procor	1979–81	Procor/various
Autic	RLS	92000–92111	PQA	SNAV, France	1979–82	Railease/various
Comtic	RLS	92300–92345	PKA	SNAV, France	1981–3	Railease/various
Carflat	MAT	94001–94135	PIW	South Staffs Wagon	1963–4	MAT Transauto
Carflat	RLS	94400–94424	PFB	Standard Wagon	1979	Railease/various

Cartics

The backbone of the car-carrying fleet is provided by the 596 Cartic wagons owned variously by MAT Transauto, Silcock & Colling, and Procor. The Cartic is a 24 t glw, open-framework, two-deck wagon, contoured to exploit every inch of the loading gauge and designed to operate in permanently-coupled four-wagon articulated sets, known as Cartic 4s. Each set is carried on five ECSS Ridemaster bogies, articulation being possible with the low weight of the loads to be carried, and desirable given the considerable cost savings per wagon. All four wagons in a set are identical except that buffers and drawgear are only fitted to the outer ends of the two 'Outer' vehicles, while on one of the two 'Inner' vehicles is carried the single brake cylinder. Drop-down flaps are provided so that loading can take place from either end and cars can be driven right through a set; special high-level ramps are needed for loading the top deck.

MAT 90215, a Cartic 'Outer', had recently been fitted with protective 'Expamet' mesh side-screens when photographed at Stoke in May 1987. The livery comprises blue bodywork and screens, with white lettering and black bogies.

The design was developed by British Railways in conjunction with the Ford Motor Company, and following the successful introduction of a number of railway-owned sets in 1964, the major car distributors began to acquire their own fleets. The largest, of some 400 wagons, is owned by MAT Transauto, the first 23 sets were built by Rootes Pressing in 1966, the remainder by Standard Wagon and BREL's Ashford works, who also built the Procor fleet. Each Cartic 4 set comprises four consecutively numbered wagons, ie MAT 90000/1/2/3, with no evidence of swapping between sets ever having been recorded. In addition to their TOPS

The Silock & Colling Cartic fleet is fitted with plastic sides and roof as shown in this study of SILC 90524, taken at Heywood in November 1985. Bodywork is orange with white lettering; bogies and roof are black and side-panels pale yellow.

numbers, these wagons also carry owner numbers, the ranges being: 401A–503D for the MAT vehicles; 0001A–0031D for Silcock's; and T/01A–T/19D for the Procor fleet hired to Toleman. Each set measures over 200 ft in length with space for 26 average-size family cars, and can run up to 75 mph allowing for very high utilization.

Unfortunately, in recent years increasing problems of vandalism and theft have prompted a programme of modifications in order to provide better protection and security to the new cars. In 1984, Standard Wagon began fitting plastic side-panels and roofs to the Silcock fleet, the roof being raised for loading by a shore-supply of compressed air, while all other Cartics have been fitted with protective 'Expamet' mesh side-screens.

Cartics appear on all significant traffics, both of home-produced and imported cars. Silcock and Toleman share the movement of all Ford vehicles, there being a considerable flow between the plants at Dagenham and Halewood, as well as to distribution centres in Scotland, South Wales and the South-west. The MAT sets can be seen virtually anywhere, but are especially common on workings from the Rover Group's plants in the West Midlands.

Procor 80

Despite the success of the Cartic, articulated vehicles have a number of inherent disadvantages; the most important is that should one wagon in a set fail, then all four are put out of use, so that when Procor unveiled a new type of car carrier in 1979, they returned to a more conventional design. The Procor 80 is a 37 t glw air-braked, open-framework two-deck bogie wagon, 76 ft long and capable of accommodating up to 10 average-size cars, although it is especially productive when loading larger saloon or estate vehicles. Sambre-et-Meuse-built Y25 bogies allow 75 mph operation, further compatibility with the existing Cartics being incorporated in the design to enable the use of existing loading facilities, though the Procor 80 has greater headroom on the lower deck, as well as shallower slopes at each end, so as to

PR 90874 demonstrates the original condition of the Procor 80. Note the hinged plates on diagonally opposite corners at both levels which form the bridge between adjacent vehicles and the loading ramp. When photographed at Longport in July 1987, this wagon carried the 'Renault' yellow livery with black lettering and bogies.

In 1986, a number of Procor 80s were sold to the Toleman Group and reprefixed accordingly. This view of TOLD 90887 also illustrates the pvc side-screens fitted to these vehicles in recent years. Body and screen are blue with white lettering on black patches and black bogies. Stoke, May 1987.

reduce the risk of damage to vehicles being driven along the wagon. Rubber bumpers are fitted to the inner faces of all vertical pillars, as the extreme length of the wagon necessitated a slight reduction in width in order to remain within gauge, while the body has staggered side pillars to allow for improved driver access to the cars and to reduce the risk of door damage.

Imported cars now take a large share of the British market and the first ten Procor 80s are hired to Renault for the onward distribution of cars brought into the country through Goole Docks. The remainder were originally hired to Toleman for carrying imported cars from the East Anglian ports to the Bathgate distribution centre near Edinburgh. As with the Cartics, the problem of vandalism has led to the need to fit protective side-screens, but because of the restricted width of the Procor 80, a rigid screen was impracticable, and therefore these wagons have been fitted with pvc mesh screens on the lower deck and pvc sheet screens on the upper deck. In 1986, PR 90883–90907 were sold to Toleman and re-prefixed TOLD.

Autics and Comtics

Hard on the heels of the Procor 80, Railease introduced another two-deck articulated vehicle known as the Autic. Built by SNAV in France, these 22 t wagons were based on a type already in operation on French Railways, and they differ from earlier designs in being three-axle, permanently-coupled two-wagon sets, sharing a central axle. At over 88 ft long, an Autic set can carry between 12 and 13 of the type of car

RLS 92097, one of the three-axle articulated car transporters, seen at Heywood in December 1987. Note the end mechanism for lowering the top-deck. The livery is orange with black stripe and lettering.

quoted in the Cartic context, but is particularly productive when loaded with small cars. One feature unique to the type is that the upper deck ends are hinged to allow loading from a single ramp, a useful facility for short-term traffics when the expense of installing a permanent high-level ramp may not be justified.

Following extensive trials with the prototype set, this type made its commercial debut in 1982 when 20 sets were hired by Cartransport, a subsidiary of the National Freight Consortium, for use between Kings Norton and Bathgate, conveying both Leyland and Talbot cars. A further 14 sets are hired to Renault and operate from Goole, with 21 sets in general service with MAT Transauto. A number of Autics have been fitted with side-panels and roofs, though the majority only have mesh side-screens.

Although two-deck wagons make good use of the restrictive British Rail loading gauge, they are unsuitable for moving lorries or other tall vehicles. Therefore in 1981 Railease introduced a second French-built design, the 24 t glw Comtic, especially for commercial vehicle traffic. Like the Autic, the Comtic is also a three-axle articulated two-wagon set, but has a single deck slung low between the axles enabling it to carry all but the tallest vehicles with space for three large lorries, or five to six small vans. As with the Autic fleet, double-link suspension was fitted, although from RLS 92330 this changed to the more robust FAT 29 suspension, earlier wagons being gradually modified to this type.

The majority of Comtic sets are hired to MAT Transauto and can commonly be seen working out of the Midlands and North-west; a few are operated by Silcock &

The single-deck equivalent of the Autic, the Comtic, is designed to carry lorries and other tall vehicles. RLS 92325, fitted with FAT 29 suspension and loaded with Leyland lorry chassis, was recorded at Warrington in April 1987. Unlike the majority of this fleet, which are painted bright yellow, RLS 92325 and its companion RLS 92324 carry an overall orange livery with white lettering on black patches, and a 'Silcock Express' nameboard in black, orange and white.

Colling, while a single set is in service with Renault working out of Goole.

Carflats

To cope with the then ever-growing traffic in motor vehicles, during the 1950s British Railways modified a considerable number of pre-nationalization coach underframes by replacing the coach body with a planked wooden floor. Low side-rails were also fitted, with drop-down flaps at each end for easy loading, vehicles being secured in position by wheel-chocks spiked to the wagon floor. In 1963, South Staffs Wagon began a similar modification of over 100 former Southern Railway coaches for MAT Transauto, additional features including the fitting of air through pipes to permit op-

eration to the Continent via the train ferry services. However, although some 63 ft long they could only carry four or five cars, and following the demise of the export car traffic they were placed in store. Recoded PFW, they have seen further occasional use, particularly when demand for the more specialist wagons has been high, and in 1984 a number were fitted with air brakes for a return to regular traffic carrying commercial vehicles.

The small batch of Railease carflats are very similar, except that being modified from redundant British Rail Mk 1 coaches, they have Mk 1 light double-bolster bogies, not the knife-edge swing-link type found on the MAT vehicles. Though air braked, they have also seen little use in the 1980s.

Chapter 7

Mineral Wagons, Opens and Tipplers

Relatively few privately-owned mineral or open wagons have been built since 1948, no doubt because British Railways followed the example of its predecessors in providing a considerable fleet of such vehicles itself. Tippler wagons, however, given their more specialized role, have been much more common in private hands.

Table 16: *Mineral wagons and opens, two-axle*

Type	Number series		TOPS code	Builder	Date	Owner/Operator
Coal	CEGB	23000–23113	PMO	Various	1937	CEGB, Midlands
Mineral	SRW	6297–6302	PMV	Standard Wagon	1981	Standard Wagon/various
Mineral	SRW	6317–6325	PMV	Standard Wagon	1981	Standard Wagon/various
Mineral	RLS	6326–6328	PMA	Standard Wagon	1981–2	Railease/various
China clay	RLS	6303–6316	PRA	Standard Wagon	1983	Railease/Wiggins Teape
Highfit	MODA	5100–5141	POV	Standard Wagon	1969	Ministry of Defence, Army
Soda ash	CCC	5500–5599	POO	C.C. Crumps	1971–2	C.C. Crumps/ICI Mond
Soda ash	CLWD	5600–5819	POO	C.C. Crumps	1975	Clwyd Wagon Co/ICI Mond
Scrap metal	RLS	5900–5980	POA	Standard Wagon	1976–84	Railease/British Steel
Scrap metal	RLS	5000–5099	POA	Standard Wagon	1984	Railease/British Steel
Scrap metal	RLS	5214–5253	POA	Various	1987	Railease/various
Scrap metal	TRL	5142–5462(r)	POA	C.C. Crumps	1985–8	Tiger Rail/various
Building blocks	PLAS	5417–5446	POA	W.H. Davis	1988	Plasmor
Scrap metal	43 70 6094 432		PIA	ANF Industrie	1956	Tiphook Rail/AS & W

Mineral wagons, two-axle

The Central Electricity Generating Board owned a large fleet of 30 t glw mineral wagons which were used to supply coal to local power stations throughout the country. Built in 1937 by G.R. Turner and the Metropolitan Carriage & Wagon Company, the CEGB's wagons were all 21 ft 6 in long, with a 12 ft 6 in wheelbase underframe fitted with shoe suspension, and a simple box-like body which could carry 20 t. In the late 1960s, the introduction of 'Merry-go-Round' coal workings to serve the new 'base-load' power stations heralded

Following their withdrawal from main-line use, a number of the CEGB 20 t mineral wagons were retained as internal-user vehicles. CEGB 23092 was recorded at Padiham Power Station on a bitterly cold day in January 1986. Livery is light grey with black markings and underframe.

RLS 6301, one of the mineral wagons built on redundant palvan underframes. This vehicle is from the first batch which have a high-sided body. Since their construction in 1981 they have been air-braked and their prefix altered to RLS. Tees Yard, September 1987.

The second batch of Railease minerals have a longer, lower body, as fitted here to RLS 6320, recorded at Tees Yard in September 1987. The livery of this entire fleet is a heavily weathered light grey with, in the majority of cases, white lettering on black patches and black running gear.

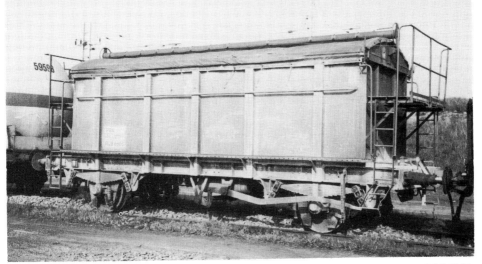

RLS 6305 was also built using a redundant palvan underframe and bears a strong resemblance to RLS 6301. However, it is additionally fitted with end platforms and ladders and a tarpaulin hood which enables its use in china clay traffic. The livery is grey with black lettering on a white panel, red hood and black underframe. Warrington, May 1987.

the demise of this fleet, the last examples being withdrawn from main-line use in 1977.

The remaining mineral wagons listed in Table 16 were all built by Standard Wagon using underframes taken from redundant APCM pallet vans. Three batches have been produced, the second having a somewhat lower and longer body than the others, though all can carry 24 t. No doors are fitted, which somewhat restricts their use, since they can only be unloaded by means of a mechanical grab or an electromagnet, and after a few years carrying agricultural lime to Scotland and scrap metal in the North-east, all were stored out of use by 1987.

Standard Wagon also built 14 similar wagons in 1983 for china clay traffic between Cornwall and the Wiggins Teape paper mill at Corpach, outside Fort William. To protect the load, these wagons are additionally fitted with roller-type tarpaulin covers, while they were fitted with air brakes from the outset to allow their use in Speedlink services.

Open wagons, two-axle

The 13 t Highfits built for the Ministry of Defence in 1963 were a direct copy of the British Railways diagram 1/044 open, featuring corrugated steel ends, five planked sides with a small drop-door in the centre, and a standard 17 ft 6 in long underframe with 10 ft wheelbase and shoe suspension. They were used on general traffic between various military installations until withdrawal in the early 1980s.

Also classed as open wagons were an interesting batch of former British Railways 16 t minerals, purchased by CC Crumps in 1971, and fitted with tarpaulin bars and plastic covers for hire to ICI Mond. They were used to carry soda ash from Northwich to a terminal at Glazebrook alongside the Manchester Ship Canal, where the load was end-tipped into waiting cargo boats for export to Africa and the Far East. In private ownership, these wagons carried an attractive livery comprising a blue body and covers with white lettering, orange solebars and black running gear; the entire fleet was withdrawn in 1979 following the ending of the export traffic.

A considerable fleet of Railease-owned open wagons has appeared since the first 51 t glw scrap metal carrier took to the rails in 1976. Built as a prototype, RLS 5900 had a tall box-like body, reinforced by vertical stanchions along the sides and ends and an 'L'-girder welded around the top lip. A small door was located in each side to facilitate cleaning out, all unloading being by electro-magnet. Ladders were provided at diagonally opposite corners to allow inspection of the load, while inside the body all 90° angles were eliminated by welding additional plates across them to prevent accumulation of scrap and to ease cleaning. The body was carried on a conventional steel channel underframe fitted with English Steel Friction Pedestal suspension units, and the original livery comprised a yellow body with black lettering and underframe. Upon completion, RLS 5900 began a series of demonstration runs visiting numerous scrapyards and steelworks throughout the country.

Although a success, experience of service conditions highlighted a number of weaknesses in the original design, and the next batch of 20 wagons, RLS 5901-5920 built in 1982, was fitted with horizontal bracing half way up both sides and ends to prevent the progressive damage caused by swinging electro-magnets which had shown up in the prototype trials. Overall length was increased from 24 ft 4 in to 26 ft 1 in, with the wheelbase extended by 1 ft to 16 ft. No ladders were fitted to this batch, which were carried on Gloucester Floating axles, while a revised livery of bright blue body

The first production batch of 20 Railease scrap carriers is illustrated by RLS 5906, seen at Heywood in October 1987. The angled steel plates along the sides and ends were added in 1985 and are designed to deflect spilled scrap on to the ground, problems having arisen when small pieces of scrap, especially 'turnings', having collected on the prominent ledges, were subsequently blown off in movement causing considerable discomfort to railwaymen working on the permanent way or to passengers waiting on station platforms. The livery comprises bright blue body sides, solebars and suspension units, with the body ends, headstocks and side top-capping angle in yellow. All lettering is white.

RLS 5040, seen passing Manchester Victoria in April 1987, is an example of the 100 Railease POAs rebuilt from 51 t hopper wagons in 1984. The additional bracing produces an unusual 'grid' pattern on the sides and ends. The livery is basically identical to that carried by the earlier batch, other than the addition of the initials 'SR' which refer to Standard Railfreight, the operating company set up to manage the POA fleet.

RLS5217, photographed when brand new at Heywood in October 1987, is an example of the 40 Railease POAs built using underframes taken from redundant 'Tip-Air' wagons. Note the revised body design to obviate the problems caused by horizontal bracing. Livery is overall black with yellow hatching along the top-capping angle and headstocks. The 'wire' symbol is in blue and red on a white patch, 'Railease' in light blue, other lettering white.

and solebar, with yellow ends and top capping, was adopted.

With government assistance in the shape of a £2.52 million 'Section 8' grant, a further 160 scrap-carrying 'POAs' were built in 1984. The first 100, RLS 5000-5099, were technically rebuilds of the BSC Ravenscraig hoppers, detailed in Chapter 2, although in practice only the underframes were re-used, lengthened to 26 ft 1 in and fitted with a new 'POA'-type body. This featured additional horizontal bracing, as well as heavier top-capping girders, and the replacement of the small side-doors

with a narrow slot which necessitated the fitting of ladders to allow access. The other 60 wagons, RLS 5921-5980, had an identical body carried on brand-new underframes fitted with Gloucester Floating-axle suspension.

Upon completion of this final batch in November 1984, the entire fleet of 181 vehicles took over all long-distance movements of scrap metal to the British Steel Corporation's works in the Sheffield and Rotherham area.

In 1987, a further batch of 40 Railease 51 t glw opens was built using underframes taken this time from redundant Tip-Air wagons. Although a new body design with more vertical stanchions was adopted, capacity remained at 32 t, and the first 20, built by Standard Wagon, were leased to Allied Steel & Wire for long-distance scrap metal traffic to their Tremorfa Works in Cardiff. The remainder, RLS 5234-5253, built by Marcroft Engineering, Coalville, were initially allocated to aggregate traffic.

Tiger Railcar's 45 t glw opens are also built on redundant tank underframes, the first ten taken from ex-ferry tanks, the remainder from former liquid chlorine and caustic soda tanks. All have a low-sided body, although, as a result of their parentage, TRL 5142-5151 present an unusual asymetrical appearance since the brake platform at one end of the original underframe has had to be retained. Since their introduction in 1985, a variety of loads has been carried, including agricultural lime, calcified seaweed and baled scrap. Plasmor, the building block manufacturer, owns a fleet of 30 open wagons which operates between Heck, near Doncaster, and depots around London. All are rebuilt from railway-owned vans with cut-down ends and special light-weight collapsible sides.

The only ferry-fitted privately-owned open wagon listed in Table 16 is a 29 t capacity vehicle owned by Tiphook Rail. Built in 1956, this wagon was used in France until 1986 when it was renumbered into the British series and allocated to scrap metal traffic in South Wales.

Table 17: *Tippler wagons, two-axle*

Type	Number series		TOPS code	Builder	Date	Owner/Operator
Ironstone	BSCO	20000–20699	PSO	Charles Roberts	1939–40	British Steel, Corby
Ironstone	BSCO	25150–25249(r)	PSO	Various	1940–73	British Steel, Corby
Ironstone	BSCO	25101–25135	PSO	Metro-Cammell	1962	British Steel, Corby
Ironstone	LW	25000–25100	PSV	Central Wagon	1962	Central Wagon/BSC, Corby
Ilmenite	BTP	24000–24600	PSO	Various	1974–7	British Titan Products
Salt/Lime	PR	25500–25523	PSA	Procor	1974–5	Procor/various
Demonstrator	RLS	5400	PSA	Standard Wagon	1982	Railease

Tippler wagons, two-axle

The first batch of British Steel two-axle tipplers listed in Table 17 was originally built for Stewarts & Lloyds to carry home-produced iron ore to their steel furnaces in Corby. These 22 t glw wagons had a distinctive body, the sides of which sloped inwards towards the solebar, but could only carry $16\frac{1}{2}$ t. Hurst Nelson and the Birmingham Carriage & Wagon Company built a further 40 tipplers in 1940 to a larger, $23\frac{1}{2}$ t capacity design, with straight sides, the majority of which survived to receive TOPS numbers in the BSCO 25150-25189 range.

In 1962, the Central Wagon Company and Metropolitan Cammell each built a batch of $26\frac{1}{2}$ t ironstone tipplers to supplement the increasingly ancient Stewarts & Lloyds fleet. Both were copies of British Railways designs, the Metropolitan Cammell wagons being built to diagram 1/183 while the Central Wagon batch had the 10 ft wheelbase underframe and vacuum brake introduced with diagram 1/185. Finally, in 1973, a number of the original 16½ t tipplers were fitted with new bodies by W.H. Davis, uprated to 27½ t, and renumbered in the BSCO 25190-25249 range. A livery of grey body and solebar, with white lettering and black running gear, was common to the entire British Steel, Corby, fleet, while examples of each batch survived in use until home production of iron ore ceased in 1978.

British Titan Products also owns a large fleet of two-axle tippler wagons which it uses to carry imported ilmenite from Immingham Docks to its factory in Grimsby. The original batch comprised some 300 wagons, the majority, 16 t minerals, acquired from British Rail, these being replaced in the late 1970s by a further batch of rebuilds, this time using shortened underframes taken from former 35 t BRTE Class B tank wagons. All had a low-sided box-like steel body, although capacity varied from 20 t with the earlier wagons to 26 t with the later rebuilds.

Procor's fleet of two dozen 24 t tipplers, which were amongst the first wagons built by the company, also use old tank underframes to which has been fitted a low-sided box-like open body. However, these 15 ft wheelbase vehicles were air-braked for their new role, and in recent years have been upgraded with either parabolic springs or FAT 26 double-link suspension. They have been operated by various companies, including Capper Pass and ICI, but since 1983 all have been concentrated in the North-east carrying agricultural lime for either Steetley Minerals or Tilling Construction.

RLS 5400 is a unique 39½ t capacity side-tipping aluminium-bodied wagon, built in 1982 as a demonstrator. Each side is made up of a full-length, top-hinged door and a smaller bottom-hinged flap, so that when the body is raised sideways, by means of hydraulic jacks, the sides swing open allowing the load to slide out. The strengthened underframe is fitted with Gloucester

British Titan Product's fleet of two-axle tipplers includes wagons of either 20 t or 26 t capacity, distinguished by the red or yellow top-capping respectively. BTP 24561, one of the 26 t wagons, was noted at Immingham in November 1986 with light grey body, black underframe and white lettering.

Pedestal suspension units and has a 16 ft wheelbase. After undergoing a series of trials with colliery waste and various quarried products, this wagon has languished out of use at Heywood, although its side-tipping design was subsequently incorporated in the Thompson bogie tipplers detailed below.

Table 18: *Open wagons and tipplers, bogie*

Type	Number series		TOPS code	Builder	Date	Owner/Operator
Pallet, open	PR	5300–5311	PNA	Procor	1977	Procor/various
Scrap metal	PR	3100–3139	PXA	Procor	1982–3	Procor/Sheerness Steel
Scrap metal	PR	3150–3159	PXA	Procor	1986	Procor/Sheerness Steel
Aggregate	PR	3140–3149	PXA	Procor	1983	Procor/Foster Yeoman
Aggregate	PR	3160–3169	PXA	Procor	1987	Procor/Foster Yeoman
Aggregate	PR	27000–27016	PXA	Procor	1986	Procor/Amey Roadstone
Concrete sections	PR	3170–3247	PXA	Procor	1987–8	Procor/TML
Minestone	TRL	3248–3267	PXA	Various	1988	Tiger Rail/TML
Ironstone	BSSC	26000–26106	PTA	BREL Shildon	1971	BSC, Scunthorpe
Ironstone	BSTE	26450–26563	PTA	BSC Dorman Long	1972	BSC, Teesside
Ironstone	BSSW	26564–26677	PTA	BSC Dorman Long	1974	BSC, South Wales
Ironstone	BSRV	26678–26850	PTA	BSC Dorman Long	1976–7	BSC Ravenscraig
Aggregate	PR	26801–26850	PTA	BSC Dorman Long	1972	Procor/Amey Roadstone
Agricultural lime	THOM	28000–28004	PTA	Standard Wagon	1985	W. & M. Thompson
Colliery spoil	BBC	28009–28012	PTA	Standard Wagon	1988	Boothferry Borough Council
In-line tippler	REDA	28100	PTA	Standard Wagon	1987	Redland Aggregates

Open wagons, bogie

The 'PN' code applies to a single batch of bogie open pallet wagons originally hired to ICI Mond to convey drums of chlorine, sulphur dioxide and 'Arcton', as well as palletized loads of cylinders and bagged chemicals, between Runcorn and Willesden. These vehicles are 59 ft 6 in long with Gloucester Fastfreight bogies centred at 42 ft 10 in, the sides being made up of five, five-plank drop-doors. When in ICI use, the central section carried purpose-built cradles and clamps designed to secure the drums of hazardous chemicals, while the livery consisted of varnished wood with white lettering, grey door hinges and ends, orange sole-bars and black running gear. In 1986, all 12 were fitted with cargo winches and modified doors to carry roofing tiles for Redland.

The remaining open wagons listed in Table 18 are all classified by TOPS as 'PX', but, as they are in effect large opens, they have been included in this chapter. Indeed, the bogie scrap carriers built for Sheerness Steel were initially allocated code 'PO', until it appears to have been decided to reserve this coding for two-axle wagons.

The 40 wagons built for use by Sheerness Steel between 1982 and 1983 appeared in two separate batches, the only difference being in the fitting of a scrap deflection plate to the ends of the first 30. All are 58 ft 6½ in

Above *Shortly after modification for Redland roof tiles, PR 5300, the first of the 70 t bogie pallet open wagons, was recorded at Acton in September 1986. Bodywork is light green with 'Redland' in red, number panel black and white, and underframe black. These vehicles carry roof tiles from Stirling to Gateshead in addition to the traffic between Brandon and Acton* (R. Silsbury).

Below *As described in the text, the bogie open wagons operated by Sheernesss Steel were originally coded POA. This branding survived on the wagons for many years as can be seen in this view of PR 3124, taken at Shipley in September 1985. Three years in scrap metal traffic have removed the gloss of the livery, which comprises a pale blue body with dark blue solebars and bogies, and black lettering. The 'Sheerness Steel' symbol is in two-tone blue on a white circle.*

long and have Schlieren M25 bogies centred at 37 ft 8¾ in. The flat-sided solebars are a distinctive feature, while the body has heavily-reinforced sides and plain ends formed from five separate horizontal sections. A small door for cleaning out is situated towards the right-hand end of each side, which is also useful for access, the ladder rungs welded on each end often being badly damaged by spilled scrap. A 73 t load can be accommodated in these 102 t glw wagons which operate from various scrapyards, particularly in Yorkshire and the Midlands, to Sheerness, normally running in Speedlink services. A daily block-train working from Ridham Dock is also operated by these wagons which avoids the use of numerous heavy lorries across the Kings Ferry Bridge on to the Isle of Sheppey.

The success of this design encouraged Procor to expand the fleet, and a further four batches of similar wagons were built between 1983 and 1987. Unlike the earlier builds, the bogies and brake gear for these later batches were second-hand, recovered from withdrawn bogie tank wagons, although the body design remained substantially unchanged.

Wagons hired to Sheerness Steel carry a two-tone blue livery with white lettering and black bogies, while those operated by Foster Yeoman, which are fitted with Association of American Railroads type automatic couplings, are painted light grey with blue and white lettering and black underframes. The fourth batch, PR 3170–3247, are also fitted with AAR-type automatic couplings for hire to Trans-Manche Link, the consortium building the Channel Tunnel, and carry concrete segments from Grain to a private siding alongside Shakespeare Cliff, near Dover. These wagons have bright yellow bodies and black underframes.

A further batch appeared in 1988 built by Procor and C.C. Crumps. Owned by Tiger Rail, they are fitted with full drawgear and buffers at each end, and are also on hire to Trans-Manche Link carrying minestone from Snowdown Colliery. Livery is royal blue with a yellow and black 'Tiger' symbol and black bogies.

Finally in this category, Procor has constructed a small fleet of 102 t glw opens for hire to Amey Roadstone. While the body design remains little changed from the

The automatic coupling and lack of buffers are evident in this photograph of PR 27001, taken at Westbury in April 1987. The bodywork is pale mustard with the 'ARC' symbol, headstocks and Schlieren bogies in grey (P. Fidczuk).

Above *PR 11304, a 102 t bogie covered hopper, seen at Ardwick in March 1986. Following the end of its use in tripolyphosphate traffic in 1986, this wagon was repainted in 'CPC' livery to carry powdered starch between Manchester and Scotland.*

Below *'Depressed-centre' Presflos have taken over the tripolyphosphate traffic between Corkickle and West Thurrock. PR 10125 was photographed at Warrington in January 1987 when stopped for repair.*

23 70 9192 002–3, one of the unusual 'Twin-Cone' cement wagons owned by Storage & Transport Systems, is seen stored out of use at Coalville in 1987.

Left *CAWD 92717, a 41 t two-axle container wagon, recorded in February 1987, when almost brand new at Radyr Yard loaded with a purpose-built coal container (A. Prime).*

Below *AVON 92564, an 80 t bogie container wagon, photographed passing Bristol Parkway in April 1987 when loaded with three refuse containers (A. Prime).*

Tyne & Wear 50 t bogie flat, TWT 95456, is one of three wagons fitted with scaffolding to assist with overhead line maintenance. The cabins are used as staff and stores accommodation. South Gosforth, August 1987.

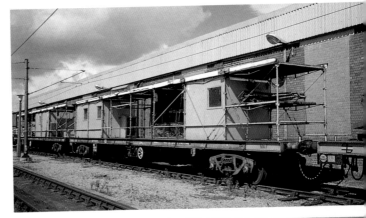

Right *In 1983, Marcon introduced a second batch of 102 t hoppers for sea-dredged gravel. MAR 17715, with end cowling and Gloucester GPS bogies, was seen at Cliffe in August 1986* (A. Prime).

Below *Another 102 t hopper used for sea-dredged aggregate, ELC 17509, also recorded at Cliffe in August 1986. Note the Gloucester Mk 4 bogies and full-length solebars* (A. Prime).

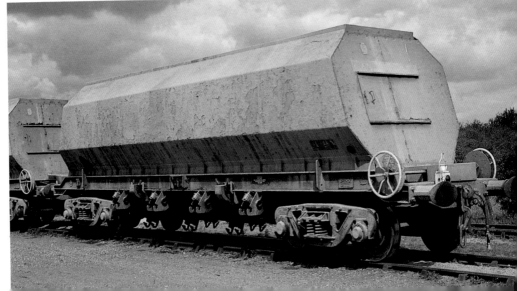

Above *BHQ 17117, a 90 t aggregate hopper built by W.H. Davis in 1986, and used to carry 'hardstone' from Bardon Hill Quarry to depots in the south. Bardon Hill, July 1987.*

Below *The small fleet of 88 t hoppers owned by Hall Aggregates carries sea-dredged gravel from Newhaven to Tolworth and Crawley. This view shows HALL 13704 waiting to be loaded at Newhaven in May 1987 (A. Prime).*

Above *THOM 28001 is one of five bogie side-tipping wagons built in 1985 for W. & M. Thompson to carry agricultural lime from Ferryhill to Montrose. It is seen at Heywood in February 1986 when returned for repair.*

Below *BRT 6904, a 46 t two-axle pallet van operated by Campbells Soups Limited. This is one of eight vans rebuilt in 1981 with curtain sides. Stoke, August 1985* (T. Mann).

One of the Procor-owned 46 t two-axle vans, PR 6919, photographed at Horbury in February 1987. The first two wagons in this batch have additional white markings along the curtain sides.

Left LS 7005, a 75 t Lloyds & Scottish bogie pallet van, was originally built with curtain sides. In 1970 it was fitted with metal cupboard doors as seen in this view taken at Radyr Yard in August 1986 (A. Prime).

Below Dow Chemicals bromine tank wagon 43 70 7490 357-0 seen at Ellesmere Port in December 1986. These small tanks operate between Amlwch and the Continent in company with similar vehicles owned by VTG.

The statutory livery applied to Class A tank wagons is illustrated in this photograph of BRT 57653, a 46 t tank recorded at Horbury in February 1987 when stored out of use.

Right The plain black livery common to most Class B and bitumen tank wagons is illustrated by BRT 57405, a 46 t lagged and coiled tank leased by Mobil. When seen at Horbury in February 1987, it had just been fitted with a new buffer.

Below TRL 51684 is one of the 46 t liquid chlorine tanks leased to ICI Mond by Tiger Rail, a type particularly common in the Northwest. Ellesmere Port, May 1987.

Above *Following a decline in traffic in the early 1980s, a number of former caustic soda tanks found other uses. TRL 51635, recorded at Ellesmere Port in December 1986, had been repainted and fitted with parabolic springs for use in Speedlink services carrying chalk slurry.*

TRL 51953 is one of a small batch of 46 t nitric acid tank wagons built to operate between Ince and Springfield. It is seen at Ellesmere Port in March 1987 when en route to the works of C. C. Crump at Connah's Quay.

Sheerness Steel fleet, apart from the omission of the small doors, these wagons are also fitted with automatic couplings in order to operate with the former iron ore tipplers also used by this company.

Tippler wagons, bogie

Three types of bogie tippler wagons have been constructed, the most numerous being a $77\frac{1}{2}$ t design owned by British Steel which at one time numbered over 400 vehicles. Following re-nationalization in 1967, the British Steel Corporation embarked upon a £3,000 million investment plan based on the use of imported iron ore. Rail was chosen to move the ore from the coastal terminals to the nearby steelworks, and as each of the four new import berths at Immingham, Redcar, Port Talbot and Hunterston came on stream, British Steel introduced a separate fleet of 102 t glw bogie tipplers dedicated to each flow.

To minimize cost, a simple, heavily-reinforced design was chosen for the wagon bodies, while to speed the unloading procedure each wagon was fitted with automatic couplings, one of which could rotate in its housing so that by passing through a special rotary dump-installation, a complete train could be unloaded without the need to uncouple any of the vehicles. A plain grey livery with white lettering was chosen for the entire fleet, although the rotary coupler ends of the wagons are painted orange for ease of identification, since trains must be marshalled in the correct order.

The first batch of 107 British Steel bogie tipplers was built by BREL for the Immingham-Scunthorpe run, and differs from all the subsequent batches in the design of the reinforcing ribs. They are 37 ft 6 in long with FBT bogies centred at 23 ft, later vehicles having BSC's own 'Axle-Motion' bogies. All remain in use, as do the South Wales and Scottish fleets operating between Port Talbot and Llanwern, and between Hunterston and Ravenscraig respectively, but following the closure of the Consett steelworks in 1981 the Teesside fleet was withdrawn and sold to Procor. After an extensive overhaul, which involved fixing the

One of the rotary tippler wagons owned by British Steel, Scunthorpe, was recorded at Immingham in September 1986. BSSC 26105 is an 'end' wagon and carries the rotary automatic couplings at the far end. The livery comprises a grey body, with the auto-coupler end picked out in orange, white lettering on black patches and black bogies (T. Mann).

The Redland 'In-line' tippler REDA 28100 seen passing through Manchester Victoria en route to Mount-sorrel in October 1987. Livery is natural metal with pale green nameplates lettered red; the underframe and hydraulic equipment is black with white lettering.

automatic couplings, they were hired to Foster Yeoman and Amey Roadstone for aggregate traffic, the wagons on hire to Amey Roadstone being renumbered in the PR 268xx series, the remainder simply receiving a change of owner prefix.

W & M. Thompson owns five 60 t bogie side-tipplers, their design having been adapted from the two-axle prototype, RLS 5400, detailed above. The bogie wagons are, in effect, two side-tipping bodies mounted on a single underframe, carried on two Y25C bogies centred at 31 ft. This small fleet operates exclusively between Ferryhill, Co Durham, and Montrose, carrying agricultural lime.

A further four bogie side-tipplers were built in 1988. Owned by Boothferry Borough Council, they carry spoil from Hatfield Colliery, near Doncaster, to a landfill site at Glews Hollow, Goole.

Standard Wagon has also built an in-line tippler, REDA 28100. This wagon also features two separate bodies mounted on a single underframe, but unlike the Thompson tipplers these are raised longitudinally by large rams situated at each end, the load being tipped through an opening in the centre of the underframe. Apart from being less likely to foul the loading gauge, this design has the advantage of being able to use existing, under-rail unloading facilities.

Chapter 8

Vans and Coaches

Upon nationalization, British Railways adopted the practice of its predecessors by constructing a large fleet of common user vans for general merchandise traffic, to which were later added a number of more specialized designs. Such provision continued well into the 1970s, and in consequence privately-owned vans have been relatively uncommon.

Table 19: *Vans and Palvans, two-axle*

Type	Number series		TOPS code	Builder	Date	Owner/Operator
Palvan	JW	6050–6069	PVV	BREL/various	1955	John Walker & Sons
Ventilated	MODA	6000–6009	PVV	Charles Roberts	1959	Ministry of Defence, Army
Palvan	MODA	6800–6815	PVB	Gloucester RC & W	1968	Ministry of Defence, Army
Palvan	APCM	6201–6296	PVV	Standard Wagon	1964–6	Associated Portland Cement
Palvan	PR	6850–6855	PVF	Standard Wagon	1968	Procor/ICI Mond
Palvan	BRT	6900–6914	PVB	Standard Wagon	1973	BRTE/Campbells Soups
Curtain-side	PR	6915–6934	PVA	Procor	1982	Procor/various
Railiner	TRL	6950	PVB	Powell Duffryn	1980	Tiger Rail/EVS
Rail van	PR	6400	PVB	Procor	1976	Procor/various

Vans and Palvans, two-axle

Johnnie Walker's small fleet of ventilated pallet vans were all originally railway-owned vehicles, built in 1955 at British Railways' Faverdale and Ashford works to diagram 1/211 as part of a much larger construction programme which had begun in 1953. This first pallet van design, while retaining the then standard 10 ft wheelbase underframe, differed markedly in appearance from earlier vans so as to accommodate the increasingly popular palletized load. Body sides and ends were of plywood panels, strengthened with steel angles and vertical and diagonal tee-sections, but the most unusual feature was the provision of double hinged-doors, located at the extreme left-hand end of each side, which gave an 8 ft 5 in wide opening to allow entry by fork-lift truck. Unfortunately, the design was not a success as continued loading caused severe wear, making them unstable at speed, and by the mid 1960s increasing numbers were being withdrawn following an alarming rise in the incidence of derailments.

In 1967, John Walker & Sons purchased 20 such vans for use on a restricted working, carrying casks of blended whisky from their blending plant at Barleith to their bottling plant in Kilmarnock, a distance of only four miles. No modifications were undertaken whilst the vans were in private hands, apart from renumbering and the addition of large advertisement boards, and all were finally made redundant in 1981 when a new blending plant was constructed in Kilmarnock. Subsequently, a number of vans were donated to railway preservation societies at Dalmellington, Ayrshire, and at the Bridge of Dun, near Montrose.

Another small fleet of vans was that owned by the Ministry of Defence for carrying government stores to various depots throughout the country. The first ten vehicles, MODA 6000–6009, built in 1959 to British Railways diagram 1/208, were standard 12 t ventilated vans with corrugated steel ends, wooden planked sides, and plywood cupboard doors positioned centrally in each side. The 17 ft 6 in long, 10 ft wheelbase underframe had shoe suspension and vacuum brakes. The remaining 16 vans were built in 1968 to a specialized design, featuring a 25 ft 6 in long, all-metal body reminiscent of a British Railways gunpowder van but with a 16 ft wheelbase underframe with double-link suspension and air brakes. Capacity was doubled to 24 t, and, while the entire fleet was out of use by 1984, a couple of the later batch survive in internal use at Eskmeals and at Long Marston.

Standard Wagon has built three batches of pallet vans, beginning in 1964 with 96 vehicles for Associated Portland Cement, originally numbered BV1–96. The gradual improvement in pallet van design was

JW 6060, a former BR palvan, recorded in Scotland in the late 1970s. Apart from the addition of the TOPS number plates and the company sign-boards to the sides, these vans remained in their original condition when in private hands (J. Walker & Sons).

Associated Portland Cement's No BV 069, photographed at Hoo Junction in 1968. This wagon was subsequently numbered APCM 6269 and carried an attractive livery of grey roof and body with black lettering, and black underframe with white lettering. The central name-panel comprised a blue circle with a yellow edge, white circular lettering and centre, and red 'CMC' initials; smaller brand names were red on yellow (D. Larkin).

reflected in these vehicles which were fitted with double-link suspension and an extended 16 ft wheelbase to improve the ride characteristics, though somewhat surprisingly they only received vacuum brakes. Access was by means of double doors located centrally on each side, which were arranged to move outwards before sliding back to give a 9 ft wide opening within the 25 ft 6 in overall length. Body sides and ends were of plywood panels, strengthened with steel angles and tee-sections.

At 36 t glw, these vans could carry $22\frac{1}{2}$ t of bagged cement and were used by Associated Portland Cement for nationwide distribution, working out of its plants at Northfleet and Snodland in Kent.

However, by 1982 a decline in demand for cement, coupled with the increased popularity of cement movement in bulk, led to a number being sold back to Standard Wagon for modification into other types, the remainder going into store at Blue Circle plants in southern England to await a decision on their fate. In 1986, two vans were fitted with air pipes for trial running in Speedlink services, but this experiment was not followed up and all the survivors were withdrawn in 1987.

In 1968, Standard Wagon built a second batch of vacuum fitted, 36 t glw pallet vans, all six surviving in Procor ownership to receive TOPS numbers. All were rebuilt from twin drop-side wagons, with two large wooden sliding doors per side, each fitted with heavy horizontal and vertical bracing. At 23 ft 8 in they were slightly shorter than the APCM vans, but could carry 25 t, although their 15 ft wheelbase underframes were only fitted with shoe suspension. All six were withdrawn in 1985 after spending a number of years in internal use at ICI's Willesden terminal in North London.

Standard's third design of two-axle pallet van, which appeared in 1973 for wagon hirers BRTE, was a 46 t glw vehicle mounted on BSC Friction Pedestal suspension units, with clasp air brakes and an unusually long 22 ft wheelbase allowing a top speed of 75 mph. Four wooden sliding doors made up the full 34 ft 6 in length of each side, the two central doors set slightly outboard of the others to allow access to the entire internal area for loading by fork-lift truck, while the ends were strengthened by two vertical and one horizontal stanchions.

Following the testing of BRT 6900 at Derby, after which International screw couplings were fitted in place of the original Instanter type, all 15 of these vans entered service between Kings Lynn and Scotland on behalf of Campbells Soups Limited. This traffic marked a welcome return, for after a highly-publicized commitment to rail in the 1950s, the disenchanted soup manufacturers had decamped to road transport by 1965.

Although in general a success, difficulties were sometimes encountered with these vans should a pallet of tinned produce shift during transit, thus jamming the sliding doors. Therefore, in 1981 eight had their doors replaced by curtain-sides. This entailed fitting a single curtain, made of woven polyester sheet coated with pvc and lacquer, to each side, the top being mounted on nylon runners and the bottom tensioned, so as to be load-bearing, by 17 fastening straps. Once the modified

vehicles had returned to traffic, the remaining seven vans were withdrawn.

A somewhat similar batch of 20 curtain-sided vans appeared from Procor in 1982, although at 41 ft 9 in over the headstocks they are considerably longer than the BRTE vans. Vertical strengthening stanchions are carried on the end, while the one-piece curtain-sides are tensioned by 20 fastening straps; the 29 ft 6 in wheelbase underframe is fitted with FAT 28 friction-link suspension. After an initial period in store, these vans have carried various commodities, including bagged cement, fertilizer, and foodstuffs.

Tiger Rail's solitary curtain-sided van, known as the 'Railiner', was built as a speculative venture using the underframe from a redundant cyclohexane tank. At 35 ft long, TRL 6950 can carry 29 t, and has a 19 ft wheelbase underframe fitted with double-link, auxiliary spring suspension. Upon completion in its distinctive yellow and black livery, it entered service in Cornwall carrying bagged china clay.

The remaining two-axle pallet van, PR 6400, was a unique 51 t glw prototype, introduced by Procor in 1976 with the intention of maximizing the payload of palletized products in a vehicle that provided full access. This was achieved by forming each side of the van from a combination of four small cupboard doors, and two larger sliding panels, with each panel located between two of the cupboard doors; the two central doors were hinged to their adjacent panels, so that when opened they formed a single sliding unit. By opening the doors and sliding the panels in various different ways, it was possible to provide access to one-half of the side, or to produce a central opening some 17 ft 3 in wide. The body sides were of ribbed metal sheet, each door having its own locking bar, while the ends carried substantial vertical stanchions. The

35 ft 1 in long underframe had Gloucester Floating-axle suspension units, with a 20 ft 9 in wheelbase, the maximum load being 37 t.

After a few years trial service with Wm Cory & Sons, when it is thought to have carried a blue and white livery, PR 6400 was repainted brown and yellow and leased to Ben Chairs (Western) Limited. It remained in use with Ben Chairs until 1986, carrying contract furniture from Frome, Somerset,

to various destinations in the more distant parts of the country, including Glasgow and Newcastle. Unfortunately, a number of problems beset this operation, the most serious being as a result of the inherent weakness in the design of the van's sides, which were twice damaged whilst passing other trains in the Severn Tunnel. After a few months in store at Healey Mills yard, Wakefield, PR 6400 was withdrawn during 1987.

Table 20: *Vans, Palvans and coaches, bogie*

Type	Number series		TOPS code	Builder	Date	Owner/Operator
Palvan	LS	7001–7050	PWA	Various	1968–75	Lloyds & Scottish/UKF
Palvan	BRT	7150–7168	PWA	Various	1972–5	BRTE/UKF Fertilizers
Palvan	SSTR	7300–7324	PWA	Procor	1975–6	UKF Fertilizers
Weed Control CC		99007–99015	PWV	Various	1931–50	Chipmans Chemicals
Weed Control FA		99900–99906	PWV	Various	1936–57	Fisons Agrochemicals
Escort Coach	MODA	99150–99151	PWV	Various	1958–9	Ministry of Defence, Army
Ferry Van		33 70 2797 000–029	PIA	BREL Shildon	1979	Danzas
Ferry Van		83 70 2795 300–349	PIA	L. H. Busch	1986	VTG
Ferry Van		83 70 2795 350–364	PIA	Wagon Union	1987	Transfesa

Palvans, bogie

Nationwide distribution of fertilizer from the UKF plant at Ince, Cheshire, began in 1968 using a fleet of 30 75 t glw curtain-sided bogie pallet vans, built by the Gloucester Railway Carriage & Wagon Company. Owned by wagon hirers Lloyds & Scottish, they were purpose–built for Shellstar, as the fertilizer company was then known, and at 45 ft 3½ in long carried 48 t on 16 specially designed pallets. Unique features included an intermediate floor for ease of stacking, as well as dunnage bags to prevent the load from moving in transit. Each end carried four angle supports as well as levers used to raise the roof when loading, the vans riding on Gloucester

Fastfreight bogies centred at 32 ft, and the underframe having side-trussing between the bogies on which was carried all the wagon details. The original Shellstar livery featured blue curtain-sides, with yellow 'Shell' and 'star' symbols, the ends, roof, and underframe being painted black with white lettering.

A second batch of 18 vans was constructed for Lloyds & Scottish in 1971 at BREL's Ashford works, slightly longer than the earlier vans, and fitted with four pairs of metal cupboard doors per side. The underframe details and ends remained unchanged, although the roof was now fixed, and the body painted light grey with white lettering. In 1975, this batch received

TOPS numbers in the LS 7031–7048 range, while the earlier vehicles, which had been rebuilt with metal doors in 1971, became LS 7001–7030. A further 18 all-steel fertilizer vans were built at Ashford in 1972, identical to the previous batch apart from the fitting of Gloucester GPS bogies to BRT 7167, and the use of an overall brown livery.

The third generation of UKF pallet vans appeared from Procor in 1975, similar to the Ashford-built vehicles but with a slightly simplified end and without the underframe side-trussing. Capacity remained at 48 t, though with this batch a new brown and white livery was adopted, all earlier vans eventually being repainted in these colours. Following a serious collision at Bridgwater in 1974, two vans, LS 7013 and BRT 7151, were written off, their replacements, LS 7049 and BRT 7168, being built by Procor in 1975 using bogies recovered from the damaged vehicles, while the remaining van, LS 7050, an ex-perimental 49 t capacity vehicle incorporating stainless steel doors and a flat roof, was built that same year by W.H. Davis.

Since 1984, a number of the earlier UKF vans, particularly those showing severe signs of wear, have been fitted with new doors, including an experimental gull-wing door conversion to LS 7029. The doors swing upwards, and are therefore less prone to damage, although they are designed to be opened and closed by fork-lift trucks, the hydraulic jacks being only intended for use in an emergency.

Coaches, bogie

In addition to the bogie pallet vans operated by UKF Fertilizers, a number of old coaches sold into private hands were also included in the 'PW' category. The majority are used on weed control duties, both Chipmans and Fisons operate two weedkilling trains which visit most parts of the rail network at least once a year. Each train com-

LS 7050, the unique stainless steel palvan built by W.H. Davis, was photographed at Ince in November 1984. The doors have a natural metallic finish with brown ends, roof and underframe. The 'horse and thistle' symbol is in black and white, 'UKF' in brown, and 'Fertilisers' green on a white patch. Other lettering is white.

Fisons Agrochemicals own a number of vintage coaches including FA 99902, a former Great Western Collett brake, built at Swindon in 1937, which has been modified for use as a stores van in the weedkilling trains. When photographed at Castleton in August 1987, it had been recently repainted emerald green with a white stripe at waist level, grey roof and black bogies; lettering is yellow. However, these vehicles quickly become stained with the chemicals being sprayed.

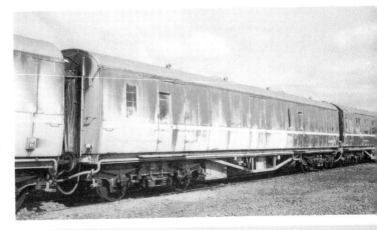

As the weedkilling trains may be away from their home base for long periods, a Staff and Dormitory vehicle is provided. One such vehicle, FA 99904, an ex-LMS corridor third built at Derby in 1946, is shown at Castleton also painted in the new green livery. Note the pipe mounted along the solebar which carries water from the tank wagons to the spray coach.

FA 99900, one of the two spray coaches owned by Fisons Agrochemicals, photographed at Castleton in August 1987. This particular vehicle is unique in having been converted from a former Gloucester RC & W Co diesel multiple unit coach, built in 1957. Note the spraying nozzels, fixed to the solebar beneath the modified double-window, and the retention of the end windows, useful when the weedkilling train is being propelled. The green livery is accompanied by yellow ends on this vehicle.

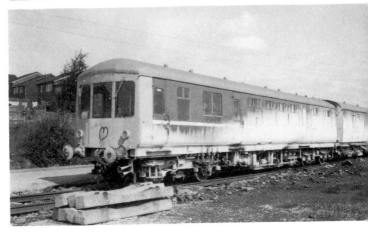

prises two or three tank wagons loaded with water, together with three or four coaches, one of which is fitted with spraying equipment, the others being used to store the special chemicals and for staff accommodation. All the Chipmans coaches are of former Southern Railway design, while Fisons own a selection of mainly Great Western and LMS vehicles.

Finally, two British Railways Mk 1 Brake Second Corridor coaches were sold to the Ministry of Defence in 1963 for use as escort vehicles, both being dual braked in 1983, and at the same time recoded in the 'PP' category, along with the weedkilling coaches.

Ferry vans, bogie

High-capacity ferry vans have become an increasingly common sight on British Rail since the late 1970s, and although the majority are foreign-owned, three batches of bogie vans have been registered in Britain. The first, built in 1979, comprises some 30 vans owned by Danzas, a Swiss-based freight forwarding company, which uses them to carry general merchandise and palletized goods between Britain and Italy, three sliding doors on each side providing access to one-third of these 54 t capacity vehicles at a time. The ends and roof are blue, the sides being left in a natural metallic finish, as is common with many sliding-door vans, with black and blue lettering, and black underframe.

Vereinigte Tanklager und Transportmittel Gmbh, a West German concern, also owns a fleet of British registered bogie ferry vans, introduced in 1986. Built by Link Hoffman Busch, these 90 t glw vehicles can load up to an impressive 63 t, each side being formed of two large sliding panels allowing access to one-half of the van at a time.

Transfesa, a Spanish-based company which specializes in the transportation of fresh fruit and vegetables, has also introduced a small fleet of 90 t glw sliding-wall vans for traffic between Britain and the Continent.

Chapter 9

Miscellaneous and Special Wagons

All privately-owned wagons that do not readily fit into one of the other categories are classified in the 'Miscellaneous & Special' group and coded 'PX'. This coding, therefore, covers a selection of vehicles of widely differing types, from the massive 'Liquid Steel Torpedoes' to the diminutive barrier and match wagons, with each batch of wagons often consisting of but a handful of vehicles.

Table 21: *Miscellaneous and special wagons, two-axle*

Type	Number series		TOPS code	Builder	Date	Owner/Operator
Tube	BSCO	4000–4019	PXV	Standard Wagon	1966	British Steel, Corby
Tube	BSCO	4241–4260	PXV	Standard Wagon	1966	British Steel, Corby
Tube	PR	4201–4240 (r)	PXF	Standard Wagon	1968	Procor/ICI Mond
Rod coil	RLS	4300	PXV	Standard Wagon	1981	Railease
Barrier	RLS	4900–4917	PXA	Standard Wagon	1980	Railease/ICI Mond
Match	PR	4918–4919	PXQ	LMS, Derby	1947–9	Procor
Match	LT	95800–95801	PXQ	BREL Ashford	1961	London Transport Board
Spacer	BSTE	4951–4956	PXQ	BREL Shildon	1969	British Steel, Teesside
Runner	BTDH	4981–4982	PXV	BREL Shildon	1957	British Transport Docks, Hull
Runner	ABP	95030–95031	PXV	Various	1950–7	Associated British Ports, Humber
Training tank	SUKO 50000		PXV	Metro Cammell	1964	Shell (UK) Oil
Dummy flask	CEGB 91100		PXW	BREL Shildon	1959	CEGB Midlands
Nuclear flask	NTL	95750–95751	PXA	BREL Ashford	1970	Nuclear Transport Limited
Ramp	MODA95000–95004		PXP	SR, Ashford	1940–1	Ministry of Defence, Army

Tube and rod coil wagons, two-axle

The 40 wagons owned by British Steel's Tubes Division, Corby, were originally built for timber traffic, being sold to British Steel in 1971 after their previous owner, J.H. Davies, had ceased to use rail. All were 27 ft 1 in long with a 14 ft wheelbase, standard shoe suspension and could carry $22\frac{1}{2}$ t. In British Steel ownership they ran in

A rebuilt British Steel, Corby, tube wagon, BSCO 4254, seen at Stoke in June 1985. Livery is light grey body and stanchions, black underframe and white lettering.

block-train formations loaded with steel tubes from Corby to various steel stock-holders in the West Midlands.

In 1975, in order to accommodate larger tubes, 20 wagons were lengthened to 32 ft $1\frac{1}{2}$ in and uprated to $23\frac{1}{2}$ t. This rebuild was undertaken by Standard Wagon and involved increasing the length of the solebars, floor, and brake linkages, the original ends being retained unchanged, while the eight stanchion pockets were repositioned with wider spacings along the edge of the solebar. In 1974, the 20 original vehicles were given TOPS numbers in the BSCO 40xx range, the rebuilt wagons being numbered in the BSCO 42xx range. By 1985, consideration was being given to air piping this fleet, but in the event all 40 were withdrawn from main-line use in 1986 and the tube traffic was transferred to railway-owned air-braked wagons.

Also classified as tube wagons were the three dozen Procor-owned 36 t glw opens that survived to be given TOPS numbers in the range PR 4201–4240. These were 23 ft

8 in long, twin drop-side vehicles, their 15 ft wheelbase underframes being fitted with shoe suspension and AFI vacuum brakes. All were leased to ICI Mond and carried cylinders of dangerous chemicals between Runcorn and Willesden until the introduction of the air-braked pallet opens, PR 5300–5311, in 1977, when they were withdrawn from main-line use.

The single rod coil wagon, RLS 4300, was built as a prototype in 1981 using an underframe taken from one of the APCM pallet vans. However, it was not a success and had been withdrawn by 1984.

Barrier and match wagons, two-axle

Railease own a batch of 18 purpose-built barrier wagons which are all hired to ICI Mond and accompany trains of hydro-cyanic acid tanks when the latter operate on the main line. All are 32 ft 10 in long with FAT 24 taperleaf suspension and a 20 ft 9 in wheelbase. RLS 4900–4905 have the

RLS 4915, one of the 14 t Railease barrier wagons fitted with high ends. The bodywork is grey with white lettering and a black and white number panel. Solebars and headstocks are red with black lettering and the running gear is black. Billingham, September 1983 (R. Silsbury, by kind permission of ICI plc).

appearance of flat wagons with a large weight carried in the centre of the floor, while RLS 4906–4917 are additionally fitted with large, high ends to provide protection against possible spillage of this highly dangerous chemical. These vehicles normally run in pairs — usually one of each type — and can be found at either end of a train of tank wagons, separating the locomotive and the brake van from the dangerous load.

When vehicles fitted with non-standard

Procor-owned match wagon PR 4919, recorded at Tinsley in September 1986. This former LMS brake-van carries a somewhat untidy bauxite livery with black and white number panel and various instruction panels in red and white. The underframe is black with white lettering (T. Mann).

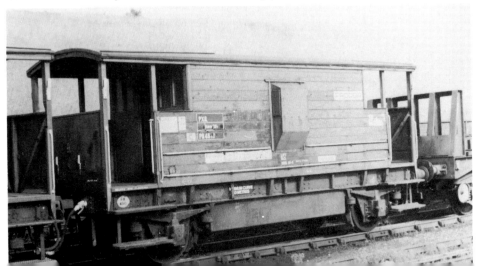

couplings are required to run on British Rail, it is usually necessary to accompany them with barrier or 'match' wagons, that is vehicles fitted with conventional buffers and drawgear at one end and a compatible non-standard coupling at the other. The majority of match wagons are railway-owned but two such vehicles, both ex-LMS 20 t brake-vans, were sold to Procor in 1986. After being refurbished and fitted with air pipes, they have been used to accompany Procor-owned tipplers and hoppers fitted with AAR couplings to and from works.

In 1961, BREL Ashford completed the final lot of standard British Railways 20 t brake-vans built to diagram 1/507. They were immediately followed by a further six vans to the same design, ordered by London Transport for use on departmental trains. During 1980, two of these vans, B 583 and B 584, were converted by W.H.

Davis to surface-stock match wagons with the fitting of a through air pipe and a buckeye coupling at one end. Both vans are based at West Ruislip and are allocated TOPS numbers LT 95800 and LT 95801 respectively, their main use being to assist in the disposal of withdrawn underground stock to scrap merchants in the Rotherham area.

Spacer and runner wagons, two-axle

In 1969, the British Steel Corporation's Northern and Tubes Group began a movement of hot metal in specially designed 'Torpedo Wagons' between Cargo Fleet, near Middlesbrough, and Consett. As each 'Torpedo Wagon' weighed in excess of 240 t when fully loaded, spacer or runner wagons were required between one 'Torpedo' and another, in order to separate

ABP 95030, the steel-bodied 'Lowfit', used at Immingham Docks. Recorded in November 1986, its livery is a rusty brown with white lettering on black patches.

the load and distribute the weight. Initially, six brake-vans were modified for this role, all bodywork being removed and a through air pipe fitted in addition to the hand-brake which was retained. However, these vehicles were not a complete success and by 1976 they had been replaced in the 'hot metal' trains by railway-owned, air-braked, 32 t glw coal hoppers.

Associated British Ports, previously known as the British Transport Docks Authority, have owned a handful of former British Railways wagons, including two vacuum-braked single bolsters converted from 'Lowfits', which were used as under-runners with their bogie bolster wagon, BTDH 3500. In 1984, two more 'Lowfits' were purchased, again for use as runners, both having been left in their original condition, ABP 95030 with steel sides, having been built at Shildon in 1957 to diagram 1/002, and ABP 95031 retaining its wooden sides, having been built at Wolverton in 1950 to diagram 1/001. They run in company with bogie bolster ABP 2100, and are used on track maintenance work in the Immingham Dock complex.

Training wagons, two-axle

One of the most unusual of all special wagons is SUKO 50000, the 21 t glw LPG Training Vehicle. Originally a 45 t glw Class B tank wagon, SUKO 64214, it is no longer authorized to carry a load, having been modified in 1981 to provide a mobile training vehicle for staff involved in the handling of liquid petroleum gas. Internally, the tank has been fitted with the complex pipework normally found in LPG wagons, access for instruction being provided by a door in one end. Externally, the wagon has lost its top-hatches, catwalk and end-ladders, but gained a side-hatch, again for instruction purposes. The 15 ft wheelbase underframe has also been modified to allow the vehicle greater operational flexibility, being fitted with air pipes in 1982 and parabolic springs in 1986. The tank livery is white with a red and yellow 'Shell' symbol with black lettering and underframe.

CEGB 91100, the Central Electricity

The modifications undertaken for its role as an LPG Training Tank are clearly evident in this view of SUKO 50000, taken at Heywood in December 1987. The tank has been painted white with red and yellow 'Shell' symbol and black lettering, while the underframe remains black with white lettering.

Generating Board's dummy nuclear flask wagon, is another training vehicle, having been modified from a former British Railway's 'Flatrol' EAC, built in 1959 to diagram 2/530. Purchased by the CEGB in 1983, this 21 t wagon is now fitted with a special cradle to house the dummy flask, but otherwise remains largely unaltered with vacuum brakes and through air pipe. It is used to assist the training of Electricity Board and railway personnel in loading and unloading nuclear flasks and can be found, therefore, at any of the nuclear power station sites around the country.

Nuclear flask wagons, two-axle

The vast majority of nuclear flask wagons are bogie vehicles, often of considerable size, but in the early 1980s British Rail converted two 31 t glw air-braked double bolsters to nuclear flask carriers for use on a special movement of imported flasks to Sellafield. The conversion involved replacement of the wooden floor with one of stainless steel to aid decontamination, and the addition of flask locating brackets and a removable cover. The FAT 7b British Rail Longlink suspension remained unchanged, as did the livery of bauxite above the solebar and black below.

In 1981, the first of these two wagons, 400004 built to diagram SA 001B, was sold to Nuclear Transport Limited and renumbered NTL 95750, while 400181, built without a through vacuum pipe to diagram SA 001A, followed in 1983, becoming NTL 95751. Both were withdrawn from mainline use in 1987.

Ramp wagons, two-axle

The only two-axle ramp wagons to have operated on British Rail are an interesting fleet of five 11¾ t glw vehicles owned by the Ministry of Defence and introduced during the Second World War. All were 17 ft 6 in long and had a standard 12 ft wheelbase underframe fitted with shoe suspension, and a flat wooden floor. However, they were not designed to carry any load, but rather for use as an emergency loading or unloading ramp where no fixed facilities existed.

When being used in the ramped position, one of the axle-sets would be removed and the hinged buffers at both ends swung outwards, thus allowing one end of the wagon floor to rest on the ground and the other to be positioned hard against an adjacent railway vehicle. All five were built with through vacuum pipes and at least one also received a through air pipe before withdrawal in the early 1980s. Running gear was painted black, the solebars dark green with white lettering.

Bogie bolster and bogie steel wagons

All privately-owned bogie bolster wagons listed in Table 22 were formerly railway-owned vehicles, purchased essentially for local workings once they had become redundant on British Rail.

British Steel have owned two dozen such vehicles, which were acquired between 1964 and 1969 and used to move steel billets between their various plants in the Rotherham area until withdrawal in the late 1970s. BSRO 1000–1007 were rebuilt from War Department Warflat wagons, being 40 ft long with diamond-frame bogies centred at 30 ft and a carrying capacity of 51 t. The other 16 wagons were all former Bogie Bolster Ds, dimensionally identical at 52 ft long, with bogies centred at 40 ft and a carrying capacity of 42½ t. BSRO 2008–2015, built at BREL's Derby and Wolverton works to diagram 1/470, had LMS diamond-frame bogies and five fixed

Table 22: *Miscellaneous and special wagons, bogie*

Type	Number series		TOPS code	Builder	Date	Owner/Operator
Bogie bolster	BSRO	1000–1007	PXO	Various	1940–45	British Steel, Rotherham
Bogie bolster	BSRO	2000–2015	PXO	Various	1949–50	British Steel, Rotherham
Bogie bolster	BTDH	3500	PXO	Metro Cammell	1953	British Transport Docks, Hull
Bogie bolster	ABP	2100	PXV	BREL Lancing	1959	Associated British Ports, Humber
Bogie steel	PR	3000–3007	PXA	Procor	1974	Procor/Sheerness Steel
Steel coil	PDUF	3008–3052	PXA	Powell Duffryn	1986–8	Powell Duffryn/various
Steel coil	33 70 5899 000–104		PIB	L.H. Busch	1979	VTG
Curtain roof	33 70 4746 100–199		PIA	Arbel-Fauvet Rail	1987	Tiphook Rail/various
Linercrane	F	93100	PXA	R. Blatchford	1984	Freightliners Ltd
Ramp	MAT	94105–94147(r)	PXW	MAT	1963	MAT Transauto
Torpedo	BSTE	95701–95706	PXA	Distington Eng	1969	British Steel, Teesside
Hot ingot	BSRO	95650	PXO	Distington Eng	1969	British Steel, Rotherham
Hot ingot	BSSC	95651–95652	PXO	Int Combustion	1971	British Steel, Scunthorpe
Atomic flask	BNFL	95760	PXA	Standard Wagon	1958	British Nuclear Fuels
Atomic flask	21 70 0998 000–005		PIA	BREL Ashford	1977	British Nuclear Fuels
Atomic flask	33 70 9986 006–008		PIA	BREL Ashford	1982	British Nuclear Fuels
Road-Railer	MODA95780		PXV	Head Wrightson	1963	Ministry of Defence, Army
Nuclear flask	MODA95781		PXA	W.H. Davis	1983	Ministry of Defence, Army
TT bogie	TN	95901–95905	PXA	Gloucester C & W	1986	Trailer Train
TT adaptor	TN	95951–95952	PXA	York Truck & Eqpmt	1986	Trailer Train
TT trailer	TN	96001–96004	PXA	York Truck & Eqpmt	1986	Trailer Train

ABP 2100, a former Bogie Bolster D, was purchased by Associated British Ports for use in the Immingham Dock complex where it was photographed in November 1986. It retains its original bauxite livery with the new lettering added in white on black patches (T. Mann).

bolsters, while BSRO 2000–2007, built at the Teesside Bridge Engineering Works, Darlington, to diagram 1/472, had LNER-type diamond-frame bogies and adjustable end bolsters. Livery of this entire fleet was black with white lettering.

ABP 2100 was also a former Bogie Bolster D, built to diagram 1/478 with vacuum brakes and British Railways plateback bogies. It was purchased in 1984 to replace the slightly smaller BTDH 3500, for use on track maintenance work within the Immingham Docks complex, BTDH 3500 having been a Bogie Bolster C, built to diagram 1/471 with GWR plateback bogies and a $30\frac{1}{2}$ t carrying capacity.

Bogie steel wagons PR 3000–3007 were built in 1974 to carry finished steel products from Sheerness. They were 51 ft long with Gloucester Mk 2 bogies centred at 37 ft $8\frac{3}{4}$ in and a carrying capacity of $77\frac{1}{2}$ t. In appearance they resembled the bogie steel wagons, then recently introduced by British Rail, having the same high ends and a deep channel solebar between the bogies, but with a flat floor and six permanent stanchions along each side.

Unfortunately, this design was not a complete success, as the high ends restricted the length of steel rod that could be carried, and in 1981 the first four were converted by Procor into open wagons, with the addition of solid sides and additional diagonal bracing to supplement the original stanchions, which were retained. These four wagons then acted as prototypes for the fleet of purpose-built scrap carriers that appeared from Procor in 1982 (see Chapter 7); PR 3004–3007 remained in their original condition, though confined to local workings on the Isle of Sheppey, until they also were converted in 1985. In original condition, these wagons had grey ends and stanchions, a blue solebar and black running gear. Lettering was white, with the Procor symbol in red, white and black, and the Sheerness Steel emblem in two-tone blue on a white ground.

Steel coil wagons, bogie

Powell Duffryn's fleet of 75 t steel coil wagons are purpose-built to carry finished steel, a market in which the most stringent

---

PDUF 3027, one of the Powell Duffryn 'Structureflex' hood bogie steel coil wagons fitted with solid ends, is seen at Warrington in October 1987. The livery of the wagon is black, whilst the hood is a royal blue, with black and blue markings on white patches.

quality requirements apply, as any signs of rust or impact damage would render a coil useless. The wagons are 53 ft 1¾ in long and are fitted with Gloucester GPS bogies, the coils being carried longitudinally in a well running almost the entire length of the floor. For protection from the elements, Powell Duffryn chose to fit a sliding, 'Structureflex' hood, both to save weight and for ease of maintenance. The majority of this fleet is hired to British Steel and runs in dedicated Steel Sector services from South Wales to the Midlands, as well as handling coil traffic through Hamworthy Docks, near Poole.

Also intended for finished steel coil are the 58 t telescopic roof vehicles owned and operated by VTG. Built to UIC standards, and designed for through working to the Continent, these wagons are fitted with three steel sliding hoods, thus enabling up to two-thirds of the vehicle to be accessible at one time, as well as providing substantial protection for the coil, though with a certain loss of payload as against later designs. Five coils can be accommodated, carried in wells in the wagon floor, each fitted with a fold-over flap which supports the coil when open and provides a flat floor when closed. In addition to continental traffic, these wagons are a common sight on various internal services within Britain and can be seen in some numbers in all the major steel-producing areas.

Curtain-roof wagons, bogie

Sliding-roof types are not confined, however, to steel coil carriers, for the Tiphook curtain-roof wagons have a similar design, albeit somewhat modified to suit the more general role intended for these 65½ t vehicles. These wagons feature a flat floor with high solid ends, protection for the load being provided by a one-piece canvas tilt hood which can be folded towards the centre of the vehicle to permit easy unloading. In the closed position, the sides are load-bearing so that a wide variety of traffics can be carried, including reeled paper, sawn timber and palletized goods. Livery comprises an off-white canvas hood with blue and orange Tiphook logo, white lettering, blue ends and solebars and black bogies.

Tiphook 90 t curtain-roof wagon 33 70 4746 113–8, photographed at Willesden in August 1987 when brand new. In addition to palletized loads, these wagons also carry steel coils, mounted in removable cradles, and can be fitted with internal side webbing to handle non-palletized general merchandise (R. Silsbury).

Crane wagon, bogie

F 93100 is a prototype 66 t glw semi-motorized container transfer wagon built by R. Blatchford of Midsomer Norton in 1984. Commonly known as the 'Linercrane', this vehicle is designed to lift 20–40 ft long ISO containers to and from adjacent rail wagons and road trailers, and can be used wherever there are two parallel tracks. To unload a container, the 'Linercrane' is first driven alongside, and, once its four stabilizing legs have been lowered, the main end-jibs are then raised and extended so as to span the adjacent track. Once attached, the container can either be lowered on to the deck of the crane, for movement to another location on site, or transferred directly to a waiting road trailer. The 'Linercrane' is also capable of shunting a fully-loaded Freightliner set, power being drawn from a 150 hp Rolls-Royce diesel engine mounted between the frames. The various operations are controlled from a small cabin located at one end of the vehicle, which is carried on Gloucester GPS bogies centred at 46 ft 9½ in.

Following delivery in 1985, F 93100 was sent to the Bristol Freightliner Terminal for extensive trials, with a view towards the establishment of a number of low-volume container handling sites where the investment required for a permanent crane could not be justified.

Ramp wagons, bogie

To assist in the loading of Cartic wagons (Chapter 6) at locations where the provision of a permanent ramp would be impracticable, MAT Transauto rebuilt six carflats, MAT 94105/7/8/24/37/47, into mobile ramp wagons, fitting a collapsible ramp on top of the wooden floor. Examples can be found at various car terminals including Bathgate and Leith, both near Edinburgh.

Torpedo ladle wagons (hot metal)

The heaviest vehicles to have run on British Rail were the six 246 t glw 'Liquid Steel Torpedo Wagons', owned and operated by British Steel. As already mentioned, they were introduced in 1969 by BSC's Northern & Tubes Group in order to increase the steel-making capacity at Consett and could carry 130 t of hot metal, although this was restricted to some 100 t when working between Cargo Fleet and Consett.

Built by Distington Engineering of Workington, these wagons, which were 84 ft 8 in long, 13 ft 4 in high and 9 ft wide, had a massive cylindrical body which tapered at each end over the two-part articulated bogies, each of which had seven axles in an unusual 4 + 3 arrangement, and was fitted with equalizing link suspension and single pipe air brakes. Each wagon was fitted with four brake cylinders and two distributors, located within insulated metal boxes situated at each end of the vehicle, while a fully protected cabin, housing the ladle tilt-drive mechanism, was positioned over one of the main trunnions.

Given their considerable weight and size, severe route restrictions were applied to these vehicles, loaded wagons *en route* to Consett having to travel via Ferryhill, Leamside and Gateshead, without exception. Furthermore, trains were limited to a maximum of three 'Torpedo Wagons', plus the appropriate number of spacers, and a maximum speed of 20 mph loaded, 35 mph empty, was also imposed, whilst to guard against possible locomotive failure, and the danger of the hot metal solidifying as a result of any extended delay, a pair of English Electric Type 3 diesel locomotives were diagrammed for these workings.

By the early 1970s, these wagons also worked from Hartlepool to Consett, being

This 1969 view shows three of the massive 246 t 'Torpedo Ladle Wagons', including the eventual BSTE 95703, being shunted into the unloading shed at Consett Steelworks after the inaugural working from Cargo Fleet. By 1976, the original maroon and black livery had been replaced by one of yellow with black stripes, although the 'torpedo' and running gear remained silver and black respectively (Cumbria Engineering).

finally withdrawn from main-line use in 1981 in line with the run-down of Consett.

Hot ingot wagons

Also built by Distington Engineering was the single 107 t glw hot ingot transfer wagon, owned by British Steel, Rotherham. This wagon had a 23 ft 6 in long flat floor, supported by very deep, heavily reinforced frames, on which could be loaded a 66 t steel ingot, and a specially-shaped, removable cover, which measured some 11 ft 9 in above rail height. The wagon was fitted with two four-wheel primary coil suspension bogies centred at 15 ft 6 in, but had only a hand-brake, its operation being restricted to a maximum speed of 20 mph.

Two further hot ingot wagons, both owned by British Steel, Scunthorpe, were built in 1971 by International Combustion Limited. At some 40 ft long and 13 ft 6 in high, they were much larger than the earlier vehicle, and could carry 73 t, the centre of the floor being enclosed by a heavily insulated box-like structure resulting in a glw of 127 t. Two four-wheel BSC 'Axle-Motion' bogies were fitted, centred at 30 ft, but there was no continuous brake as the wagons were restricted to a maximum speed of 10 mph, when loaded, and 30 mph when empty.

All three hot ingot wagons were very restricted in their operations, being confined to inter-works transfer movements within their respective areas, which on occasion were required to traverse British Rail metals.

Nuclear flask wagons, bogie

Irradiated nuclear fuel, loaded in specially strengthened flasks, is carried by a number of bogie wagons, the majority of which are owned by British Nuclear Fuels. These include a former British Railways 'Flatrol' MCC, built originally in 1958 to diagram 2/531, and later converted to carry atomic flasks to the reprocessing plant at Sellafield. In 1982, this wagon was sold to British Nuclear Fuels and renumbered BNFL 95760, but with a payload limited to only 34 t its subsequent use has been very restricted.

In addition to handling the irradiated fuel from Britain's own nuclear power stations, BNFL also reprocesses spent fuel from European and Japanese reactors. Foreign flasks arrive in Britain at BNFL's own sea terminal, situated at Ramsden Dock, Barrow-in-Furness, from where they are transported to Sellafield using a small fleet of purpose-built 160 t glw well wagons. Built in 1977 and mounted on two pairs of four-wheel Y25C bogies, these six vehicles have massively-constructed side-frames supporting the floor, which drops down between the bogies to form a well capable of accommodating either a single 100 t cylindrical flask, or two smaller 50½ t square flasks. All six were built to UIC standards and carry 12-digit numbers, though in fact they rarely leave the Cumbrian Coast line. A further three wagons, uprated to 176 t glw to handle even heavier flasks, were purchased by BNFL in 1982.

The Ministry of Defence owns and operates two wagons within this category including MODA 95780, which at 86 ft 0½ in long is one of the largest private-owner wagons to have run on British Rail. This 188 t glw giant is mounted on two special 12-wheel bogies, and with its massive side-frames somewhat resembles a British Railways transformer wagon. Air brakes were added in 1984 and this wagon can normally by found in the company of the two escort coaches mentioned in Chapter 8. Livery is blue with black running gear.

The second wagon, MODA 95781, is a much smaller, more conventional flask carrier, mounted on two four-wheel Y25C bogies, and can carry a 57 t load.

Trailer Train

Trailer Train is one of the most interesting, and potentially important, developments to have appeared on the Railfreight scene. One disadvantage of using rail is that distribution can often involve the transfer of goods between rail and road vehicles, which not only takes time but can also prove costly if items are damaged in the process. During the early 1960s, an attempt to overcome this problem was developed in the USA in the form of a road/rail vehicle, but although the 'Roadrailer', as it became known, was trialed in Britain, a commercial service was never introduced.

However, in 1986 Tiger Railcar Leasing revived the idea when it unveiled the prototype vehicles for Trailer Train, a somewhat different bi-modal concept to 'Roadrailer' in that the road trailers do not carry rail wheels, which would otherwise reduce their payload and which was one of the main disadvantages of the earlier system. Basic hardware comprises a conventional 21½ t road trailer, the roof-line of which is chamfered to fit within the railway loading gauge. Below its rear doors the trailer carries a socket and locking pin, a matching tongue being fitted at the front. On the road the trailer is hauled by a conventional tractor, but to take to the rails the only facility needed is a flat section of track flush with the road surface.

On arrival at the road/rail interchange, the driver backs the Trailer Train vehicle

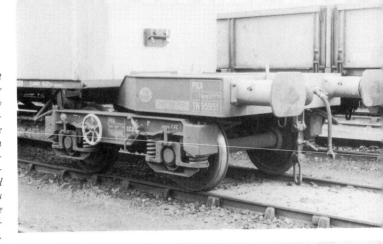

Trailer Train is one of the most original prototypes to appear for many years, one of its many unusual features being the individual numbering of separate components. This close-up, taken at Whitemoor in June 1987, illustrates two of the three basic components, bogie TN 95902 and adaptor TN 95951. The bogie is black with white lettering; the adaptor is black with a yellow bufferbeam and white lettering (A. Prime).

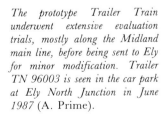

Road/rail trailer TN 96002 photographed in rail mode at Whitemoor in June 1987. The basic livery is a mid-grey van body, with 'Trailer Train' symbol in lighter grey, red and white, and the number panel in black with white lettering (A. Prime).

The prototype Trailer Train underwent extensive evaluation trials, mostly along the Midland main line, before being sent to Ely for minor modification. Trailer TN 96003 is seen in the car park at Ely North Junction in June 1987 (A. Prime).

over a rail bogie before the air suspension is used to raise the road wheels, lowering the trailer on to the bogie. The trailer's landing legs are then lowered, the tractor unhitched and driven away. When the next trailer is on its bogie, the tractor driver reverses until the socket on its rear casting engages with the matching tongue on the front of the vehicle already on the rails. When the last trailer is attached, another bogie, fitted with a special adaptor carrying conventional drawgear, supports the front of the leading vehicle and couples it to another wagon or locomotive. Unusually, each separate component, Gloucester GPS bogies, adaptors, and trailers, carry a separate TOPS number, and following an initial period of development and modification, the prototype train began running extensive trials early in 1987.

Chapter 10

Tank Wagons of below 40 tonnes glw

Tank wagons have traditionally been privately owned, since the nature of their loads normally makes them unsuitable for a common-user approach, and in consequence the type has always been amongst the most common of privately-owned wagons. Although the majority of small tanks built prior to 1957 had been withdrawn before the complete implementation of TOPS, a number of elderly fleets did survive for a few more years and have been included here for completeness, alongside the more modern designs.

Table 23: *Petroleum product tanks, 20–39 t glw*

Type	Number series	TOPS code	Builder	Date	Owner/Operator
Class A	ESSO 43200–43299	TSV	Powell Duffryn	1958–62	Esso Petroleum
Class A	ESSO 44087–44188	TSV	Various	1961	Esso Petroleum
Class A	ESSO 44253–44424	TSV	Various	1962–3	Esso Petroleum
Class A	ESSO 45001–45350	TSV/F	Various	1963–4	Esso Petroleum
Class B	ESSO 43300–43999	TSV/F	Various	1957–62	Esso Petroleum
Class B	ESSO 44189–44252	TSV/F	Various	1958–62	Esso Petroleum
Class B	ESSO 44601–44774	TSV	Charles Roberts	1958	Esso Petroleum
Class B	GULF 40127–40147	TRO	Various	1953–6	Gulf Oil
Class B	BRT 47149–47188	TSV	Hurst Nelson	1958–9	BRTE/Berry Wiggins
Class B	BRT 47200–47296	TSV	Various	1959–62	BRTE/Berry Wiggins
Class B	TEX 47761–47900	TSF	Various	1960–61	Texaco
Class B	CEGB 48500–48549	TSV/F	Various	1959–62	CEGB, Midlands
Bitumen	BRIG 40016–40024	TRO	Various	1931–51	Wm Briggs & Sons
Bitumen	BRIG 47083–47116(r)	TRO	Various	1933–55	Wm Briggs & Sons
Bitumen	BRIG 47098–47099	TSO	P.W. Maclellan	1948	Wm Briggs & Sons
Bitumen	BBES 40036–40037	TRO	Hurst Nelson	1948	British Bitumen Emulsions
Bitumen	LION 47723–47747	TSO/V	Various	1948–62	Lion Emulsions
Bitumen	RRL 48121–48126	TSV	Charles Roberts	1958–62	Retread Roads
Bitumen	ESSO 43146–43199	TSV	Charles Roberts	1958–63	Esso Petroleum
Bitumen	ESSO 44425–44494	TSV	Various	1963	Esso Petroleum
Lubricants	LP 47748–47760	TSF	Charles Roberts	1963	Lubricant Producers
Lubricants	SUKO 47720	TSF	Charles Roberts	1963	Shell (UK) Oil
Lubricants	BPO 48460–48461	TSF	Charles Roberts	1963	BP Oil

Petroleum product tanks, Classes A and B, 20–39 t glw

The importance of the 35 t glw vacuum-braked tank design developed by Charles Roberts and introduced by Esso in 1957 has already been discussed in Chapter 1. This design, which allowed a payload of 23½ t for Class A products (the lighter, highly inflammable liquids with flash–points below 23°C, such as motor spirit and naphtha) and 23 t for Class B products (the heavier, less volatile liquids, like derv and fuel oil), quickly became a standard, and was ordered in such numbers by Esso that various batches were built by other manufacturers in addition to Charles Roberts, including Powell Duffryn and Metro Cammell. However, all batches had a common 15 ft wheelbase and a riveted steel underframe fitted with roller bearings and vacuum brakes to allow 60 mph block-train operation, while the tank was of all-welded construction and was secured to the underframe by four small anchor angles. The Class B tanks were fitted with heating coils at one end in order to deal with the more viscous liquids which often require heating to effect their complete discharge.

Construction of this design continued until 1963 when Esso introduced their first 'monobloc' tank wagons, ESSO 44365–44424, again developed in collaboration with Charles Roberts. Further construction, shared by Powell Duffryn and Norbrit Pickering, increased this type to some 410 vehicles, all Class As with a capacity of 24 t. This increase was achieved through the use of the 'monobloc' principle which involved dropping the chassis crossmembers below the level of the solebar and shaping them to support an arc of the tank circumference, enabling a larger diameter tank to be fitted. The tank is then permanently attached to the underframe along its entire length by means of wing plates, welded to the top of the solebar, which are bolted to a stalk of T-section which runs the full length of the barrel and is continuously welded to it. Use of this design necessitated replacement of the side-ladders, found on earlier tanks, with a single end-ladder, while minor refinements of the underframe culminated in the adoption of eyebolt suspension and the AFI vacuum brake.

The statutory livery of silver tank with black lettering and red solebar was carried by all Esso Class A tanks until the early 1960s, when silver was dropped in favour of light grey. No statutory livery is imposed for Class B tanks, but, like the majority of other operators, Esso painted their fleet black, the only sensible colour because of the problems associated with spillage on any other livery. All lettering was white, and, in common with the Class A tanks, the Esso logo in red, white and blue was carried on an oval steel plate fixed to the side of the tank.

The majority of the Esso fleet survived into the 1980s and could be seen throughout the country working from their refineries at Fawley and Milford Haven, as well as from coastal terminals at Bowling and Tynemouth. However, closure of the Miford Haven and Tynemouth sites, coupled with a dramatic fall in the demand for heating oil and an increasing use of pipelines, had resulted in their wholesale withdrawal by 1984, although a number have been sold to other companies, such as Chipmans Chemicals, for further use.

Gulf Oil began operating in Britain in 1960 with a small fleet of second-hand, unfitted 14 t anchor-mounted tanks. They had steam coils and were used to carry fuel oil from various terminals situated alongside the Manchester Ship Canal. Unusually for Class B tanks, they were painted blue with orange lettering, the underframe black with white lettering.

The remaining Class B tanks listed in Table 23 were all built to the 35 t glw design of 1957 and included a large number owned by BRTE and built by Charles Roberts, Powell Duffryn and Hurst Nelson. All were hired by Berry Wiggins, a small oil producer with a refinery at Kingsnorth, Kent, and operated to destinations in Somerset and Gloucestershire until the traffic was transferred to road in 1975. Livery was over-all black with white lettering.

The Texaco tanks were originally operated by Regent, a joint British subsidiary owned by Texaco and Chevron, and worked from storage depots in South Wales and Avonmouth. They initially carried the red, white and blue Regent badge, but by 1967 Regent had ceased to exist and the emblem was changed to the red and white Texaco symbol. However, by 1981,

The development of the 35 t vacuum-braked tank was of major importance in the history of the private owner wagon. Illustrated is Class B anchor-mounted tank, Regent No 435, recorded at Stewarts Lane in 1973. Although owned by Texaco, this fleet retained its Regent numbers until the implementation of TOPS when this particular wagon became TEX 47885. Livery was plain black with white lettering (D. Larkin).

CEGB 48501, an ex-Esso 35 t tank sold to the Central Electricity Generating Board in 1979. This particular wagon is both lagged and coiled. The overall livery is black with white lettering, although traces of the original red, white and blue Esso transfer could still be seen when photographed at Stoke in June 1986 (T. Mann).

when Texaco all but abandoned rail, most were in plain black livery.

Finally in this category are the 50 Class B tanks purchased from Esso by the Central Electricity Generating Board in 1979, which are held on stand-by to supply coal-fired power stations with fuel oil for starting purposes in case of emergency.

Bitumen tanks, 20–39 t glw

Bitumen, the main residue produced in oil refining, began to find increasing popularity as a coating for road surfaces in the 1940s, and most oil companies use rail to transport this particularly viscous commodity.

Wm Briggs & Sons was a small company based in Dundee which owned a varied fleet of 14 t and 20 t bitumen tanks. The majority were built by Hurst Nelson with 10 ft wheelbase, unfitted underframes, the tanks being lagged to ensure the bitumen remained warm during transit. In 1979, the company was taken over by Tarmac and the bitumen tanks withdrawn, although for many years their use had been confined to the north-east corner of Scotland. Another Scottish company, British Bitumen Emulsions, also owned two 14 t bitumen tanks

ESSO 44476, a 35 t bitumen tank refurbished in 1983 with air brakes and FAT 26 suspension, is seen at Exeter Riverside in October 1987. Note the flame tubes fitted in the end of the barrel, a feature common to all modern bitumen wagons, and the hazard warning transfer placed in a prominent position on the vehicle's side. Such 'Hazchem' labels are carried by all wagons involved in the transport of dangerous goods, and indicate both the nature of the load and its attendant hazards. The livery is a badly-stained black with white lettering, the 'Hazchem' label being predominantly orange (P. Fidczuk).

which were used in the Glasgow area until the late 1970s. Livery of both these fleets was over-all black with white lettering.

The first five Lion Emulsion tanks, LION 47723–47727, which were all built in 1948, though by four different manufacturers, were $20\frac{1}{2}$ t saddle-mounted vehicles carried on 10 ft wheelbase steel underframes, the remainder of their TOPS numbered fleet having been acquired from Esso in the early 1970s. All-yellow ends enhanced the plain black livery on a number of these wagons, which operated from Warrington to depots at Hereford and Bangor until 1981. The six bitumen tanks owned by Retread Roads were also former 35 t glw Esso Class B tanks. They ran in company with the Lion fleet until the late 1970s.

Finally in this group, Esso owned a number of 35 t glw bitumen tanks built to a modified design with eyebolt suspension in place of the earlier shoe, and flame tubes in each end of the tank to enable rapid discharge. Capacity of these tanks was $22\frac{1}{2}$ t, a number being refurbished in 1983 for further use in Speedlink services between Fawley and Plymouth.

Lubricants tanks, 35 t glw

Although lubricating oils are commonly carried in Class A tanks, Lubricant Producers, a specialist company based in Manchester, owned a fleet of purpose-built 35 t glw 'monobloc' tanks introduced in 1963. All were vacuum-braked with eyebolt suspension and a 15 ft wheelbase. After the company had been absorbed by Shell Mex & BP in 1975, a few were renumbered, but all retained the somewhat unusual livery of maroon tank with white lettering and black underframe until withdrawal in 1984.

Table 24: *Pressurised gas tanks, 20–39 t glw*

Type	Number series	TOPS code	Builder	Date	Owner/Operator
LPG	ESSO 43101–43140	TSV	Various	1963	Esso Petroleum
Chlorine	AO 47000–47005	TSO	Charles Roberts	1940	Associated Octel
Chlorine	AO 47006–47042	TRO	Various	1940–58	Associated Octel
Chlorine	BPCM 47130–47148	TRO/P	Various	1950	BP Chemicals, Murgatroyd
Chlorine	ICIM 47403–47562(r)	TSO	R.Y. Pickering	1955	ICI Mond
Chlorine	ICIM 47417–47555	TRO	R.Y. Pickering	1942–54	ICI Mond
Arcton	23 70 7392 000–007	TIQ	R.Y. Pickering	1954	ICI Mond
Arcton	23 70 7392 021–026	TIQ	R.Y. Pickering	1954	ICI Mond

Liquid petroleum gas tanks, 36 t glw

Although strictly speaking intended to carry petroleum products, the liquefied petroleum gas tanks have been included in Table 24 since LPG must be transported under pressure to prevent it vapourizing. Therefore, LPG tanks are designed as pressure vessels and differ markedly from other petrol tank wagons in that there is only a side loading/discharge connection and no ladders or catwalk. The first LPG tanks were introduced by Esso in 1963, being built by Powell Duffryn and Charles Roberts to a 'monobloc' design with a capacity of $19\frac{1}{2}$ t, the tanks being carried on

15 ft wheelbase, vacuum fitted under-frames.

Chlorine and Arcton tanks, 20–39 t glw

Chlorine gas is also transported as a liquid under pressure and three similar fleets of elderly tanks lasted into the early 1980s. As chlorine is a dense liquid, only a small tank is required, the majority being 14 t capacity mounted on 10 ft 6 in wheelbase unfitted steel underframes, the tank itself being supported by either a saddle or cradle mount with large end stanchions and diagonal stays extending to the top of the solebar. To guard against end damage, wooden blocks were fitted to each end while the top filler was enclosed by a secure cover, necessary precautions given the highly toxic nature of the load.

These tanks were wide ranging and could be found in all the major industrial centres until the late 1970s when they were replaced by more modern vehicles. However, the 14 t chlorine tanks owned by Associated Octel remained in use until 1984, having been fitted with through air pipes for running between Ellesmere Port and Amlwch, in North Wales.

Arcton is a generic name used to cover a group of chemicals, most common of which is dichlorodifluoromethane, used in the manufacture of foam and produced at ICI's Runcorn works. In 1954, ICI introduced a small batch of ferry-fitted $16\frac{1}{2}$ t tanks for this commodity, the wagons being similar to chlorine tanks of the period but with air pipes, chaining-down lugs and a brake platform at one end for continental working. The initial livery comprised the statutory white tank with red bands towards each end, but by 1979, when these vehicles were air braked, this had changed to white with a broad horizontal orange stripe.

Acid tanks, 20–35 t glw

In the course of the Second World War, the Ministry of Supply purchased a large number of unfitted 14 t cradle-mounted tank wagons, primarily from Charles Roberts, the majority of which were used to carry nitric acid. In addition, a number of 15 t anchor-mounted tanks, MODA 40297–40344 range, were acquired from Germany in 1945, also for carrying acids. Unlike the British-built vehicles, they were fitted with Double-link suspension and had an unusual 14 ft 9 in wheelbase, though they were still unfitted. By 1981, the entire batch of MODA tanks had been withdrawn from main-line use.

Nitric acid is also used in the chemical reprocessing of nuclear fuel, and British Nuclear Fuels purchased nearly 100 tank wagons to serve their major plants at Springfield, near Preston, and Sellafield. Built between 1941 and 1959, they were a mixture of 14 t and 20 t vehicles, the majority having cradle mounts and either 9 ft or 10 ft wheelbase unfitted underframes, although BNFL 48066–48073, built in 1959 by M.W. Grazebrook, were anchor-mounted with 15 ft wheelbase vacuum-braked underframes. Shoe suspension was common to the entire fleet, as was a livery of light grey or silver tank and black underframe with white lettering. All operated from the Royal Ordnance Factory at Bishopton until the final withdrawal of the more modern tanks in 1982.

E.G. Steele's fleet of small tank wagons comprised a bewildering mixture of second-hand elderly vehicles, the majority having been 14 t and 20 t sulphuric acid tanks previously operated by such companies as Imperial Smelting. Huge gaps existed within the number series shown in Table 25, as only a handful survived in use after

1976, often as water carriers in railway weedkilling trains.

The only small hydrochloric acid tanks to receive TOPS numbers were five 14 t vacuum-piped wagons, built by Charles Roberts in 1950, and based at BP Chemical's Murgatroyd works, near Sandbach in Cheshire.

Table 25: *Chemical tanks, 20–39¾ t glw*

Type	Number series		TOPS code	Builder	Date	Owner/Operator
Nitric acid	MODA	40267–40344(r)	TRO	Various	1940–45	MoD, Army
Nitric acid	BNFL	40597–40610	TRO	Charles Roberts	1950–55	BNFL, Sellafield
Nitric acid	BNFL	48058–48073	TSO/V	Various	1951–9	BNFL, Sellafield
Nitric acid	BNF	40611–40671	TRO	Charles Roberts	1941–55	BNFL, Springfield
Nitric acid	BNF	48141–48150(r)	TRO	Charles Roberts	1941–4	BNFL, Springfield
Sulphuric acid	STL	40581–40590(r)	TRO	Hurst Nelson	1949	E.G. Steele
Sulphuric acid	STL	47926–47992(r)	TSO	Various	1949–51	E.G. Steele
Hydrochloric acid	BPCM	40043–40047	TRP	Charles Roberts	1950	BP Chemicals, Murgatroyd
Caustic liquor	BPCM	47118–47129	TSP	Charles Roberts	1950	BP Chemicals, Murgatroyd
Ammoniacal liquor	ICIM	47398–47695(r)	TSO	Various	1939–57	ICI Mond
Ammonium nitrate	FF	47351–47397	TSV	Charles Roberts	1958	Fisons Fertilizers
Solvent	BPCS	40053–47317(r)	TSO	Various	1940–52	BP Chemicals, Saltend
Solvent	BPBB	47322–47325	TSO	Various	1940–52	BP Chemicals, Baglan Bay
Solvent	STL	47967–47999(r)	TSV	Hurst Nelson	1958	E.G. Steele/Carless
Anti-knock	AO	47053–47069	TSQ	Charles Roberts	1950	Associated Octel
Anti-knock	AO	48462–48491	TSR	Charles Roberts	1954	Associated Octel
Anti-knock		23 70 7490 002	TIB	Charles Roberts	1964	Associated Octel
Anti-knock		23 70 7490 240–294	TIB	Charles Roberts	1961–4	Associated Octel
Anti-knock		23 70 7390 409–415	TIB	Charles Roberts	1964–5	Associated Octel
Ethylene dibromide	AO	47043–48428(r)	TSB	Fauvet Girel	1949–50	Associated Octel
Bromine		23 70 7392 292–294	TIW	Charles Roberts	1961	Dow Chem/Assoc Octel
Bromine		23 70 7490 000–001	TIB	Charles Roberts	1961	Dow Chem/Assoc Octel
Bromine		43 70 7490 295–360(r)	TIB	Charles Roberts	1961	Dow Chem/Assoc Octel
Bromine		23 70 7398 063–065	TIB	Waggon Fabrik	1961	VTG/Assoc Octel
Bromine		23 70 7498 005–008(r)	TIB	Waggon Fabrik	1961	VTG/Assoc Octel
Hexene		23 70 7392 400–405(r)	TIX	Waggon Fabrik	1958	BP Chemicals, Grangemouth
General purpose		21 70 0785 008–020(r)	TIQ	R.Y. Pickering	1954	ICI Mond
General purpose		43 70 7490 300–345(r)	TIW/B	Charles Roberts	1950–67	Tiger Rail/ICI
General purpose	SCC	48384–48387	TSR	M.W. Grazebrook	1953	Shell Chemicals
De-icing fluid	KILF	48128–48129	TSR	Various	1951–3	Kilfrost

Caustic liquor and ammonium nitrate tanks, 31½–35 t glw

BP Chemicals also owned a dozen anchor-mounted tanks for caustic liquor. In common with the hydrochloric acid tanks, these vehicles had a 10 ft wheelbase, vacuum-piped underframe fitted with shoe suspension, but the tank itself was considerably larger with a capacity of 20½ t.

Until the 1970s, ammonia was commonly transported in the form of ammoniacal liquor or as ammonium nitrate liquor, both much easier chemicals to handle than the highly toxic anhydrous ammonia. To supply their chemical plants in Northwich and elsewhere, ICI Mond owned a varied batch of 33 t glw tanks, the majority being anchor-mounted and unfitted. Livery was grey with white lettering, orange solebars and black running gear.

Fisons Fertilizers' fleet of 35 t glw anchor-mounted tanks were an adaptation of the standard vacuum-braked design introduced in 1957. Major differences included the fitting of larger heating coils, to prevent the ammonium nitrate from solidifying, and a slightly smaller tank than standard. When introduced in 1958, this

BP Chemicals 32 t caustic liquor tank T77, built by Charles Roberts in 1950, was recorded at Crewe in October 1969. The livery comprised a light grey tank with the BP 'shield' in green and yellow and 'chemicals' in light blue. Other lettering and underframe were black. On TOPS, this wagon became BPCM 47129 (D. Rowland).

Fisons Fertilisers ammonium nitrate tank M 12/34 recorded at Avonmouth in 1972. Eventually becoming FF 47384, the tank carried a green livery with black lettering; the underframe was black with white lettering (D. Larkin).

fleet operated in block-train formations between the various Fisons plants at Stanford-le-Hope, Immingham, Avonmouth and Widnes, but by 1984, when the last examples were withdrawn, they had all been concentrated on a regular working from Immingham to Ipswich Docks.

Solvent tanks, 20–35 t glw

Only a few tanks dedicated to solvents traffic were in use before 1977. These included a number of $20\frac{1}{2}$ t wagons owned by BP Chemicals which were used to carry acetone and ethanol between their plants in Hull and South Wales, while the remainder, numbered in the range STL 47967–47999, were standard 35 t glw vacuum-braked Class A tanks, built in 1958 by Hurst Nelson, and hired to Carless, Capel & Leonard for working out of their refinery at Parkeston Quay, Essex.

Anti-knock compound, ethylene dibromide, and bromine tanks, 34–$39\frac{3}{4}$ t glw

Associated Ethyl began to manufacture lead alkyl anti-knock compounds at Plumley, Cheshire, in 1940, and at a second, larger plant in Ellesmere Port in 1954, when the company changed its name to Associated Octel. Associated Octel also manufactures the associated chemicals, bromine and ethylene dibromide, and various tank wagons with capacities from $17\frac{1}{2}$ t to $23\frac{1}{2}$ t have been used to transport them to refineries and chemical works, both throughout the UK and in Europe.

Given the highly toxic nature of their loads, all these tanks are constructed as pressure vessels, the first batch for anti-knock being introduced in 1950 with a capacity of $17\frac{1}{2}$ t within a 32 t glw. These anchor-mounted tanks were 19 ft 6 in long with a 12 ft wheelbase and shoe suspension, the design being modified in 1954 to produce a slightly larger vehicle with a capacity of $18\frac{1}{2}$ t. The second batch were fully ferry-fitted and remained in use on continental services until the early 1980s. The remaining anti-knock tanks, all built since 1961, retain their 13-digit numbers and carry $23\frac{1}{2}$ t within their $39\frac{3}{4}$ t glw, the slightly larger tank being fixed to the underframe by full-length wing plates.

Associated Octel's 39 t ferry tank wagon 23 70 7490 257–6, used to carry lead alkyl anti-knock compounds, seen at Stoke in May 1987. The livery is a grey tank with blue and white 'Octel' symbol. The numberplate and underframe are black with white lettering and the instruction panel is yellow with black lettering.

Ethylene dibromide, added to the anti-knock fluid to act as a scavenger, has been produced at Amlwch since 1954. For some years, a small batch of French-built 35 t glw tanks were used for this traffic, having been previously in ferry use. All had 12 ft 3½ in wheelbase underframes fitted with air brakes and through vacuum pipes, finally being replaced on the Amlwch–Ellesmere Port run in the early 1980s by more modern vehicles.

Bromine is also transported from Amlwch using a small fleet of specialist tank wagons owned by Dow Chemicals and VTG. All are ferry-fitted, and apart from the first batch which were withdrawn in 1985, air-braked.

Other chemical tanks, 20–35 t glw

The few remaining types listed in Table 25 are largely general purpose tanks, in-cluding five 17 t vehicles built in 1958 by Waggon Fabrik of Germany. Owned by BP Chemicals, Grangemouth, they normally carry hexene from Holland to Scotland, but at least one example has been noted loaded with motor spirit.

ICI Mond, Tiger Rail and Shell Chemicals also owned small batches of ferry-fitted tanks which survived in use until the late 1970s carrying various chemicals such as propylene oxide, cereclor and trichloroethylene, while Kilfrost Ltd of Haltwhistle, Northumberland, operated two former British Railways 20½ t ferry tanks, purchased in 1969, to carry de-icing fluid to various destinations on the Southern Region, the fluid being used to prevent a build-up of ice on the electrified third rail. KILF 48128 was built in 1951 by Hurst Nelson to British Railways diagram 1/304, while KILF 48129 was to the larger design, diagram 1/305, constructed in Ashford in 1953. Other than a change in

21 70 0785 010–0, one of the small fleet of 20 t general purpose ferry tank wagons owned by ICI Mond, recorded when stored out of use at Stoke in May 1987. This particular wagon, which had been used to carry trichloroethylene, was in a dark grey livery with white lettering, orange solebars and black running gear.

livery to light blue with white lettering, both tanks remained in their original condition until withdrawn in the early 1980s.

Tar tanks, 22–35 t glw

Tar is a by-product obtained from coal distillation during the production of coking fuels and town gas and has a number of uses, particularly in the manufacture of pitch and various synthetic chemicals. In the early twentieth century, tar tanks were relatively common, but by 1976 only a few remained in existence, the majority owned by the National Coal Board and based at either Caerphilly, South Wales, or Wingerworth, near Chesterfield.

The NCB's Welsh fleet comprises two batches built by Cambrian Wagon, the first a 22 t cradle-mounted type built in 1939, the second a larger, fully-lagged anchor-mounted type with a limited 19 t capacity introduced in 1953. These were sup-

plemented by a handful of 14 t tanks purchased second-hand from the Bedwas coke works. All were unfitted and as such were largely confined to South Wales, supplying Caerphilly with tar from the local coke works as well as a flow of imported tar through Cardiff Docks, but even this limited use had ceased by 1982.

The remaining NCB tanks were operated by Thomas Ness, a wholly-owned subsidiary, from the Avenue Smokeless Fuels plant at Wingerworth. All were 14 t anchor-mounted wagons fitted with steam coils, but none survived in traffic after 1981.

Similarly, British Steel owned a few 14 t tar tanks for use on a local working in the Sheffield area between Orgreave coke works and the nearby chemical plant, until withdrawal in the early 1980s.

Midland Yorkshire Tar Distillers also owned a fleet of 14 t tar tanks which carried both tar and tar products from their works

Table 26: *Tar, water, milk, and molasses tanks, 20–35 t glw*

Type	Number series		TOPS code	Builder	Date	Owner/Operator
Tar	NCB	40224–40234	TRO	Charles Roberts	1930–50	NCB, South Wales
Tar	NCB	48300–48345	TSO	Cambrian Wagon	1939–40	NCB, South Wales
Tar	NCB	48354–48383	TSO	Cambrian Wagon	1950	NCB, South Wales
Tar	NESW	40345–40358	TRO	Charles Roberts	1951	NCB, (Thomas Ness), Wingerworth
Tar	BSOR	40591–40596	TRO	Hurst Nelson	1940	BSC, Orgreave
Tar	MYTK	40672–40682(r)	TRO	Charles Roberts	1952	Midland Yorkshire Tar Distillers
Water	CC	40722–40809(r)	TRO/P/V	Various	1950–57	Chipmans Chemicals
Water	CC	48111–48120(r)	TSV	Various	1958–61	Chipmans Chemicals
Water	CC	48441–48444	TSV	Various	1958–62	Chipmans Chemicals
Milk	MMB	42800–42839	TMV	W.H. Davis	1981	Milk Marketing Board
Milk	MMB	42840–42864	TRV/F	W.H. Davis	1981	Milk Marketing Board
Milk	MMB	42865	TSV	W.H. Davis	1981	Milk Marketing Board
Molasses	UM	48076–48108(r)	TSO	Various	1927–55	United Molasses
Molasses	TRL	47993–48057	TSV	Charles Roberts	1958–62	Tiger Rail/United Molasses
Molasses	DAVS	48550–48624	TSV/F	Various	1958–62	W.H. Davis/Distillers Co

at Knottingley and Four Ashes. These wagons had conventional 10 ft wheelbase underframes, but the tanks themselves were most unusual, being elliptical in cross-section. Livery, in common with all other tar tanks, was an over-all black with white lettering.

Water tanks, 23–35 t glw

Chipmans Chemicals have owned a number of small tank wagons for use as water carriers. These accompany their weedkilling trains, which spend the better part of the year visiting most lines in the south of England in a carefully controlled programme designed to check the spread of weeds and thus prolong the useful life of both sleepers and ballast. Chipmans originally operated a number of 14 t, 10 ft wheelbase, anchor-mounted tanks, built in the 1950s and painted in an attractive red livery. By 1958, these were in the course of replacement by a batch of standard

vacuum-fitted 35 t glw tanks built by Powell Duffryn and Charles Roberts, including four vehicles purchased second-hand from Esso. Livery of this second fleet was a more sombre over-all black with white lettering, and although branded 'Water Only' they have also been used on occasion to carry de-icing fluid from Haltwhistle.

Milk tanks, 25–35 t glw

The transportation of milk has long been associated with rail, the original six-wheel milk tanks being unique in that while the tank vessels were owned by private dairy companies, the underframes were railway property. Unfortunately, by 1980 all fresh milk had been transferred to road and it seemed that the days of the milk tank had ended. However, in a surprise move the Milk Marketing Board then decided to retain its own fleet of rail tanks for use in special cases of emergency, such as a

MMB 42830, one of the six-wheeled milk tanks rebuilt to provide a strategic reserve, noted at Shirebrook in November 1985. Note the off-centre filler, an indication that the original wagon, W44544, built at Derby in 1950, was one of the few to be already fitted with a sloping vessel. Livery is a bright steel tank with white lettering on blue or black patches, blue wing plates and black underframe with white lettering.

breakdown in road services.

Forty six-wheel milk tanks, already fitted with roller bearings and stainless steel tanks, were retained, being refurbished for further use by W.H. Davis who reclad and remounted the vessels by replacing the old wooden cradle mounts with more satisfactory steel webs. At the same time, all the vessels were sloped to facilitate unloading, a refinement found on only a few of the original vehicles.

In addition to the six-wheelers, 26 'new' milk tanks were ordered from W.H. Davis, employing refurbished two-axle, 15 ft wheelbase underframes recovered from redundant Class B tanks, and reclad stainless steel vessels removed from older milk tanks. All 66 wagons are now owned outright by the Milk Marketing Board, the six-wheelers coded 'TM', the remainder either 'TR' or 'TS', and are kept on stand-by at various strategic locations in the West Country including Chard and Lostwithiel.

Molasses tanks, 30–35 t glw

United Molasses, a Liverpool-based concern, owned a fleet of unfitted $20\frac{1}{2}$ t tanks built to a variety of designs, which were used to carry molasses from the sugar beet growing areas of East Anglia to its factory on Merseyside. Only a few survived into the 1970s, their place being taken by the 35 t glw anchor-mounted vehicles owned by Tiger Rail.

Built to the 1957 standard design, the Tiger Rail tanks were originally owned by Tank Rentals and a number carried petroleum products for Gulf Oil and Charringtons. However, by 1976 Tank Rentals had been taken over by Tiger Rail and the entire batch hired to United Molasses. In this traffic their attractive livery comprised red oxide tank with blue ends, black underframe and white lettering. The United Molasses initials were carried in blue on a white circle, while the old Tank Rentals insignia' was yellow with black lettering. However, in 1979 United Molasses ceased to use rail, and this fleet was then gradually withdrawn.

The final group of molasses tanks to consider in this section were all former Esso Class B vehicles built between 1958 and 1962 to the standard 35 t glw design. Acquired by W.H. Davis in 1980, they were modified for molasses traffic and hired to the Distillers Company to supply its distilleries in central Scotland. Repainted green, with white lettering and black underframe, this fleet only lasted until 1984 when the drive towards a fully air-braked network saw their replacement by a batch of 45 t glw tanks transferred from caustic soda traffic.

Chapter 11

Tank Wagons of 40 tonnes to 51 tonnes glw

The most common of all privately-owned vehicles are tank wagons within the 40–51 t glw range, for not only does this category include the numerous fleets of petroleum tank wagons, but also a large number of the more specialized tanks built for various chemical traffics.

Table 27: *Petroleum product tanks, 40–51 t glw*

Type	Number series		TOPS code	Builder	Date	Owner/Operator
Class A	ALG	49000–49005	TTV	Powell Duffryn	1964	Algeco/Carless Solvents
Class A	ALG	49057–49075	TTF	Charles Roberts	1964–5	Algeco/various
Class A	ALG	49087–49253	TTV/F	F.Y. Pickering	1965	Algeco/various
Class A	ALG	70300–70311	TUB	L.H. Busch	1976	Algeco/Esso Petroleum
Class A	23 70 7190 500–699		TIW/G	Various	1963–5	Algeco/various
Class A	BPO	37060–37365(r)	TTA	Various	1981–2	BP Oil
Class A	BPO	60160–60368(r)	TTV/F	Various	1964–5	BP Oil
Class A	BPO	60560–60760(r)	TTB	Various	1966–7	BP Oil
Class A	BPO	67060–67999(r)	TTB/A	Various	1966–7	BP Oil
Class A	BPO	68160–68674(r)	TTF	Various	1964–5	BP Oil
Class A	BRT	57080–57307(r)	TTV/F	Various	1965–6	BRTE/various
Class A	BRT	57477–57663(r)	TTB	Various	1966–71	BRTE/various
Class A	BRT	57747–57840	TTA	Various	1967	BRTE/various
Class A	CSL	74000–74029	TUA	CFMF	1980–81	Carless Solvents
Class A	CLMI	54017–54064(r)	TTF	Various	1964–5	CLMI/various
Class A	ESSO	56000–56281	TTF	Various	1965	Esso Petroleum
Class A	FINA	54701–54730	TTB	Charles Roberts	1966–7	Petrofina
Class A	GULF	54200–54241(r)	TTV	Charles Roberts	1964–6	Gulf Oil
Class A	PR	58101–58155	TTB	Standard Wagon	1968–9	Procor/various
Class A	PR	70023–70067	TUA	Charles Roberts	1972	Procor/various
Class A	PR	70098–70117	TUA	Norbrit Pickering	1974	Procor/various
Class A	RLS	55500–55509	TTA	Standard Wagon	1976	Railease/various
Class A	SUKO	60100–60259(r)	TTV/F	Various	1964–5	Shell (UK) Oil
Class A	SUKO	60500–60759(r)	TTF	Various	1964–7	Shell (UK) Oil
Class A	SUKO	67000–67959(r)	TTB	Various	1966–7	Shell (UK) Oil
Class A	SUKO	68100–68626(r)	TTF	Various	1964–5	Shell (UK) Oil
Class A	STL	55001–55055(r)	TTA	CFPM, France	1967	E.G. Steele/various
Class A	STS	53012–53061	TTV	Powell Duffryn	1963	STS/various
Class A	STS	53062–53091	TTF	Metro Cammell	1965	STS/various
Class A	23 70 7190 200–222		TIB	Various	1964	STS/various
Class A	23 70 7397 100–124		TIB	Pressed Steel	1966–7	STS/various

Type	Number series		TOPS code	Builder	Date	Owner/Operator
Class A	TEX	54800–54854	TTV	Various	1965	Texaco
Class A	TEX	54855–54869	TTB	Metro Cammell	1966	Texaco
Class A	TRL	51166	TTV	Charles Roberts	1961	Tiger Rail/Esso
Class A	TRL	51281–51298	TTV	Charles Roberts	1963	Tiger Rail/various
Class A	TRL	51382–51560(r)	TTV/F	Charles Roberts	1963–5	Tiger Rail/various
Class A	TRL	51804–51834(r)	TTA	Charles Roberts	1967	Tiger Rail/various
Class A	TRL	55510–55519	TTA	Standard Wagon	1976	Tiger Rail/Esso
Class A	TRL	70728–70733	TUA	Procor	1977	Tiger Rail/Esso
Class A	VIP	55201–55244	TTB	Standard Wagon	1966–7	VIP Petroleum-Elf Oil
Class B	ALG	49006–49086(r)	TTV/F	Charles Roberts	1964–5	Algeco/various
Class B	ALG	49254–49290	TTF	Metro Cammell	1965	Algeco/various
Class B	ALG	49317–49366	TTF/B	Various	1965–7	Algeco/Esso Petroleum
Class B	BPO	63160–63294(r)	TTA	Various	1966–7	BP Oil
Class B	BPO	63560–63960(r)	TTB	Various	1966–7	BP Oil
Class B	BPO	64160–64762(r)	TTF	Various	1964–5	BP Oil
Class B	BPO	65560–65787(r)	TTB	Various	1966	BP Oil
Class B	BPO	66060–66371(r)	TTV/F	Various	1964–6	BP Oil
Class B	BPO	73060	TUA	Charles Roberts	1972	BP Oil
Class B	BRT	57041–57193(r)	TTF	Various	1965	BRTE/Charringtons
Class B	BRT	57350–57476	TTB/A	Various	1966–7	BRTE/various
Class B	BRT	57566–57570	TTA	R.Y. Pickering	1967	BRTE/Petrofina
Class B	BRT	57664–57669	TTB	Powell Duffryn	1966	BRTE/Esso Petroleum
Class B	BRT	57851–57880	TTB	Standard Wagon	1970	BRTE/various
Class B	BRT	70500–70523	TUA	Standard Wagon	1973	BRTE/various
Class B	CGL	53701–53778	TTV/F	Various	1963–6	Charringtons Fuel Oil
Class B	CGL	70400–70409	TUB	Procor	1978–9	Charringtons Fuel Oil
Class B	CLMI	54000–54032(r)	TTF	Various	1964–5	CLMI/Esso
Class B	FINA	70900–70931	TUB	Standard Wagon	1973	Petrofina
Class B	GULF	54225–54256(r)	TTV	Charles Roberts	1964–6	Gulf Oil
Class B	HFO	53901–53958(r)	TTV	Charles Roberts	1963–6	Hargreaves Fuel Oil
Class B	PR	58061–58078	TTB	Standard Wagon	1968	Procor/various
Class B	PR	70068–70097	TUA	Various	1974	Procor/various
Class B	STL	55021–55079(r)	TTA	CFPM, France	1967	E.G. Steele/various
Class B	SUKO	63100–63250(r)	TTA	Various	1966–9	Shell (UK) Oil
Class B	SUKO	63500–63903(r)	TTB	Various	1966–7	Shell (UK) Oil
Class B	SUKO	64100–64723(r)	TTF	Various	1964–5	Shell (UK) Oil
Class B	SUKO	65500–65859(r)	TTB	Various	1966–7	Shell (UK) Oil
Class B	SUKO	66100–66351(r)	TTF	Various	1965–6	Shell (UK) Oil
Class B	SUKO	73000	TUA	Charles Roberts	1972	Shell (UK) Oil
Class B	TRL	51258–51338(r)	TTV	Charles Roberts	1962–4	Tiger Rail/various
Class B	TRL	51724–51803	TTB	Charles Roberts	1967	Tiger Rail/various
Bitumen	BPO	61560–61799(r)	TTB	Various	1966–7	BP Oil
Bitumen	BRT	57323–57344	TTF	Powell Duffryn	1966	BRTE/Mobil
Bitumen	BRT	57670–57696	TTB	R.Y. Pickering	1966	BRTE/various
Bitumen	LTD	74500–74503	TUA	Standard Wagon	1981	Lancashire Tar Distillers
Bitumen	PDUF	52000–52027	TTV	Powell Duffryn	1961	Powell Duffryn
Bitumen	PR	58001–58025	TTB	Standard Wagon	1970	Procor/Total Oil
Bitumen	PR	58910–58935	TTV	Various	1963	Procor/Mobil
Bitumen	PR	58941–58946	TTB	Standard Wagon	1971	Procor/Lancashire Tar Dist
Bitumen	PR	70118–70161(r)	TUB	Procor	1976–7	Procor/Mobil

Type	Number series	TOPS code	Builder	Date	Owner/Operator
Bitumen	SUKO 50500	TTV	Powell Duffryn	1963	Shell (UK) Oil
Bitumen	SUKO 52100–52344(r)	TTV	Powell Duffryn	1962–3	Shell (UK) Oil
Bitumen	SUKO 52400–52636(r)	TTV	Various	1970–1	Shell (UK) Oil
Bitumen	SUKO 61100–61348(r)	TTA	Various	1966–86	Shell (UK) Oil
Bitumen	SUKO 61500–61954(r)	TTB	Various	1966–7	Shell (UK) Oil
Bitumen	SUKO 62100–62239(r)	TTV	Metro Cammell	1965	Shell (UK) Oil
Bitumen	SUKO 71500–71515	TUB/A	Various	1973–80	Shell (UK) Oil
Lubricants	BPO 50160–50167	TTV	Charles Roberts	1964	BP Oil
Lubricants	LP 54506–54510	TTB	Various	1966–8	Lubricant Producers
Lubricants	SUKO 50100–50112	TTV	Charles Roberts	1964	Shell (UK) Oil
Lubricants	SUKO 65743–65747	TTB	Various	1966–8	Shell (UK) Oil
Lubricants	SUKO 65900–65911	TTB	Procor	1980	Shell (UK) Oil

Notes   Shell (UK) Oil tank wagons occupy the number range 00–59.
BP Oil tank wagons occupy the number range 60–99.
All BPO 37xxx tank wagons were rebuilt from BPO 65xxx Class B tank wagons.
In 1988, 51 tanks from the BRT 57xxx and PR 581xx series were renumbered PR 58230–58280.

Petroleum product tanks, Classes A and B, 40–51 t glw

In 1963, virtually all the major oil refiners and distributors signed long-term contracts with British Railways in which both parties agreed to the transportation of a minimum tonnage of oil products by rail. These agreements, which provided the basic assurances of supply which the oil companies were looking for, signalled the beginnings of yet another massive tank building programme.

Traffic was thenceforth to be concentrated on a selected number of modern terminals, each capable of handling 2,000 t block-trains, and the new round of construction immediately adopted the 'monobloc' principle as the best means of maximizing the available payload within the new $22\frac{1}{2}$ t axle limit, agreed in 1962.

By 1964, those orders already placed for 40 t glw tank wagons had been largely completed and from that date virtually all future construction was to the new 45 t glw standard design. This involved the use of a 'monobloc' type tank design with a capacity of approximately 30 t, and an all-welded steel 15 ft wheelbase underframe, fitted with vacuum brakes and UIC double-link suspension. As virtually all the major wagon builders were involved in constructing such vehicles, there were inevitably a number of detail differences between batches, in particular the use of either one or two end-ladders, or the adoption of the AFI vacuum brake, but the basic design remained largely unchanged until the appearance of the first 51 t glw tank wagons in 1972.

Over £10 million had been invested in new wagons and facilities by the end of 1966, but there was to be no slackening in the pace of development as that same year British Railways announced that all new construction should henceforth be fitted with air brakes.

The 45 t glw petroleum tank remained in construction until the mid 1970s, although after 1972 most new wagons were to the larger 51 t glw design first introduced by Charles Roberts in the shape of two Class B tanks for Shell Mex & BP, latterly numbered SUKO 73000 and BPO 73060.

SUKO 67953 is an example of the 46 t 'monobloc' tank built in considerable numbers in the 1960s. This wagon had been resprung and had lost its through vacuum pipe when seen at Warrington in October 1987. Statutory Class A livery comprises a grey tank with red solebars and black running gear.

Many vacuum-braked 46 t tank wagons were refurbished in the early 1980s with parabolic springs and air brakes, including ESSO 56194, seen at Ardwick in November 1986 when in lubricating oil traffic. The livery is standard Class A.

Another Class A tank fitted with parabolic springs is BRT 57203, seen at Preston in September 1987. This batch was rebuilt from caustic soda tanks following the Weaver Junction accident in 1975, being air-braked and resprung in 1986 for hire to Petrofina.

Above *PR 70026 illustrates the 51 t tank design introduced by Charles Roberts in 1972. Originally in Conoco livery, this wagon was repainted in 1986 and operates between the Humber Oil Refinery and various depots in the Midlands and North-west. Livery is a grey tank with black lettering, red solebars with white lettering and black running gear. Ashburys 1987.*

Below *SUKO 65545, another 46 t 'monobloc' tank, recorded at Buxton in May 1987. These wagons are used to carry Class B products that flow freely, such as kerosene, and, apart from the overall black livery, are identical to Class A tanks.*

However, relatively few vehicles were built to this new specification, since the $25\frac{1}{2}$ t axle limit is only permitted on the main routes, while the slump in demand following the oil crisis of 1974 left the oil companies with large numbers of redundant wagons.

Problems were also being encountered with the UIC double-link suspension fitted to existing wagons, and the late 1970s and early 1980s were therefore a period of consolidation, the only significant development being the adoption of parabolic springs for those tank wagons with a long-term future. By 1984, the majority of vacuum-braked fleets had been withdrawn, although a number of wagons, particularly those owned by Charringtons, Esso, and Gulf,

were being air-braked for further use.

Over the years a number of wagons have changed hands, in particular the former Texaco air-braked Class A tanks, TEX 54855–54869, which after a short period in molasses traffic with W.H. Davis, were resold in 1983 to E.G. Steele for hire to ICI to carry methanol, while a number of the VIP tanks, after a few years in Procor ownership, were resold in 1987 to Chipmans Chemicals to carry water.

Bitumen tanks, 40–51 t glw

Despite the downturn in demand for Class B products, traffic in bitumen has remained constant, the modern bitumen tank wagon

PR 58016, a 46 t bitumen tank leased to Total Oil, recorded at Stoke in May 1987. Note the flame tubes and single end-ladder. The livery is black with white lettering with the 'Total' symbol in blue, red, orange and white.

Left *Another Procor 46 t bitumen tank, PR 58942, one of the batch leased to Lancashire Tar Distillers. The overall livery is again black, but with yellow lettering and a black and white number panel. Preston, September 1987.*

Left *In 1986, Shell introduced a batch of 46 t bitumen tanks rebuilt from former Class B tanks numbered in the SUKO 63xxx series, with air brakes and parabolic springs. One such vehicle, SUKO 61316, was seen at Ellesmere Port in October 1987 in black livery with white lettering.*

Below left *SUKO 71500, the prototype 51 t bitumen tank, built by Charles Roberts in 1973 was also photographed at Ellesmere Port in October 1987. Note the plain, straight-channel solebar. Since 1986, the plain black livery of the Shell bitumen fleet has been enhanced by small numbered circular transfers in red, thought to indicate the grade of bitumen, in this case No 7.*

Right *The SUKO 659xx series tanks are reserved by Shell for lubricating oil traffic, and operate to various BR Traction Maintenance Depots in the north and east of the country. SUKO 65900, recorded at Tees Yard in September 1987, was converted from a Class B lagged and coiled tank in 1980.*

Lancashire Tar Distillers 51 t bitumen tank LTD 74501, seen at Preston in September 1987. This is one of four tanks used between Lindsey and Preston. The livery is black with white lettering.

being an ideal vehicle for handling this difficult commodity. Since 1962, all bitumen tanks have been built to the 'monobloc' design, the early batches from Powell Duffryn having a 24 t capacity while most later wagons have been of 46 t glw with a 29 t capacity.

By 1987, all active bitumen tank wagons were air-braked, although a handful of vacuum-braked tanks owned by Powell Duffryn remained in store in the Cardiff area, the other vacuum-fitted bitumen tanks having been withdrawn. Most numerous and wide-ranging are the tanks owned by Shell which can be found in all

parts of the country outside the South-east, all the other fleets being more restricted in their operation. In 1983, a number of Class B tanks from the SUKO 64xxx series were sold to Esso and were subsequently modified for bitumen traffic by the fitting of additional lagging and flame tubes.

Lubricants tanks, 40–46 t glw

In addition to their small fleet of 35 t glw tanks, Lubricant Producers also owned five air-braked 46 t glw 'monobloc' tank wagons built by Powell Duffryn and Charles Roberts. All carried the same

maroon livery as the vacuum-braked tanks until 1976 when they were transferred to Shell and renumbered SUKO 65743–65747. A few other 40 t and 46 t glw tanks have been allocated to lubricants traffic, but increasingly since the 1980s lubricating oils have been carried in any available tank wagon.

Liquid petroleum gas tanks, 40–46 t glw

As detailed in Chapter 10, the first liquid petroleum gas tanks were a batch of 35 t glw 'monobloc' wagons built for Esso in 1963. A similar design was adopted for all the later batches listed in Table 28, though with slightly increased capacities. Vacuum-

Table 28: *Pressurized gas tanks, 40–51 t glw*

Type	Number series		TOPS code	Builder	Date	Owner/Operator
LPG	ALG	49291–49316	TTV	Metro Cammell	1966	Algeco/BP Oil
LPG	BPO	59160–59172	TTV	Various	1963–4	BP Oil
LPG	BPO	59173–59198	TTA	Procor	1985–6	BP Oil
LPG	BPO	59560–59594	TTV/W	Various	1966–7	BP Oil
LPG	BPO	59595–59699(r)	TTA	Procor	1986	BP Oil
LPG	BRT	57577–57587	TTB	R.Y. Pickering	1967	BRTE/various
LPG	BRT	57881–57886	TTB	Charles Roberts	1974–5	BRTE/various
LPG	CLMI	54013–54016	TTV	Metro Cammell	1966	CLMI/BP Oil
LPG	ESSO	56341–56406	TTV	Various	1964–5	Esso Petroleum
LPG	SUKO	59100–59138	TTV	Various	1963–4	Shell (UK) Oil
LPG	SUKO	59400–59650(r)	TTV/W	Various	1966–7	Shell (UK) Oil
Chlorine	AO	55339–55357	TTB	Charles Roberts	1966	Associated Octel
Chlorine	TRL	51410–51434	TTV	Charles Roberts	1965	Tiger Rail/various
Chlorine	TRL	51561–51585	TTB	Charles Roberts	1966–7	Tiger Rail/various
Chlorine	TRL	51649–51723	TTB	Charles Roberts	1967–8	Tiger Rail/ICI Mond
Chlorine	TRL	70550	TUA	Procor	1980	Tiger Rail/ICI Mond
Ethyl chloride	23 70 7277 378–398		TIX	Charles Roberts	1964	Tiger Rail/Assoc Octel
Liquid gases	23 70 7277 353–377		TIX	Charles Roberts	1962	Tiger Rail/various
Liquid gases	23 70 7492 367–369		TIB	Charles Roberts	1962	ICI Agricultural Div
Anhydrous ammonia	STS	53250–53264	TTF	Metro Cammell	1965	STS/ICI Agricultural Div
Anhydrous ammonia	TRL	51450–51538	TTV	Charles Roberts	1965–6	Tiger Rail/ICI Agricultural Div
Anhydrous ammonia	ICIA	54301–54413(r)	TTV/F	Charles Roberts	1965–6	ICI Agricultural Div
Carbon dioxide	STS	53200–53218	TTV	Motherwell Br Eng	1962–6	STS/Distillers Co
Carbon dioxide	STS	53219–53249	TTB	Fauvet Girel	1970–71	STS/Distillers Co
Carbon dioxide	STS	53265–53283	TTB	Fauvet Girel	1974–8	STS/Distillers Co

Notes ICI Agricultural Division ferry tank wagons, 23 70 7492 367–369, were originally owned by Tiger Rail and numbered in the series 23 70 7277 353–377.
STS 53265–53276, carbon dioxide tanks built in 1974, were originally numbered STS 53427–53438.

BPO 59184, an LPG tank built by Procor in 1986 by placing the barrel of an old LPG wagon on to a redundant air-brake underframe. Note the lack of ladders and the central loading-hatch, with its sliding cover open. The statutory livery for pressurized gas tank wagons comprises a white barrel with an orange horizontal stripe at waist level. The 'BP' symbol is green and yellow, and other lettering black. The underframe is black with white lettering. Stoke, May 1987.

fitted, 15 ft wheelbase underframes remained standard while the tanks themselves could be distinguished from other petroleum wagons both by their livery and by the lack of ladders or catwalks, all loading and unloading being through valves located in the side of the barrel.

Demand for propane and butane has steadily increased in recent years, and the majority of LPG tanks listed in Table 28 had been air-braked by 1986, many also being resprung as part of a general refurbishment programme which also saw a number of former Shell-owned vehicles transferred

British Railway Traffic & Electric Co LPG tank BRT 57581, also recorded at Stoke in May 1987 but stored out of use. Originally operated by Mobil between its refinery at Coryton and the Henry Wiggins depot in Hereford, the majority of this batch were leased by Esso in the 1970s. The livery is white with an orange stripe, 'BRT' symbol in red, black and white, and lettering and underframe in black.

Above *Prominent in this view of Associated Octel 46 t liquid chlorine tank wagon AO 55351, is the end brake platform, a legacy of the vehicle's days in continental traffic. Otherwise it is a standard modern tank for chlorine traffic with central ladder, over-ride protection, and enclosed top-filler. The tank and wing plates are white, with an orange stripe and black lettering. The 'Octel' symbol, mounted on a separate metal plate, is blue and white, the instruction panel is yellow and black, and the underframe black with white lettering. Ellesmere Port, May 1987.*

Below *TRL 51416 is an example of the initial bath of Tiger Rail liquid chlorine tanks which were leased to ICI Mond and then BP Chemicals before their transfer to Hays Chemicals in 1985. The orange and white tank livery is enhanced by the 'Hays Chemicals' lettering in blue, and an orange solebar. Other lettering and running gear is black. Warrington, November 1987.*

to BP. BP Oil also added to their fleet in the mid 1980s by purchasing the entire batch formerly owned by Algeco as well as a number of rebuilt ethyl chloride tanks, formerly owned by Tiger Rail.

Chlorine tanks, 46–51 t glw

All modern chlorine tank wagons are built to a similar design introduced by Charles Roberts in 1965, and feature a relatively small tank barrel fixed by means of full-length wing plates to an air-braked, 15 ft wheelbase steel underframe. Steel buffer over-ride protection plates are carried at each end, while the batch owned by Associated Octel are additionally fitted with an end brake platform, having been used on continental services until 1982 when they were renumbered and allocated to the Ellesmere Port to Amlwch service.

The entire Tiger Rail fleet was initially hired to ICI Mond, but by 1983 the first batch had been transferred to BP Chemicals for use out of their plant at Sandbach. By the early 1980s, an increasing number of chlorine tanks were stored out of use including the solitary 51 t glw wagon, TRL 70550, while those vehicles that remained in traffic underwent a general programme of refurbishment which included removal of the through vacuum pipe and the fitting of parabolic springs.

Ethyl choride and other liquid gas tanks, 40 t glw

Ethyl chloride, butadiene, and various anhydrous amines are also transported by rail as liquids under pressure. The 40 t glw tank wagons used for these commodities were all constructed by Charles Roberts in the 1960s and closely resemble LPG tanks. However, as they were intended for continental working they were all ferry-fitted with an end brake platform, and a sun-

23 70 7277 354-0 is one of a small batch of liquid gas tanks leased by ICI's Petrochemicals Division. Of particular note is the sun-shield and end platform, although this particular wagon is used to carry butadiene to Kings Lynn. When photographed at Stoke in October 1986, the statutory livery of orange and white tank was enhanced by black lettering, an 'ICI' symbol and yellow and black 'TRL' insignia.

shield to take account of the extended journey times involved.

This additional weight limited capacity somewhat, to $15\frac{1}{2}$ t in the case of the ethyl chloride tanks leased to Associated Octel, and to 20 t in the case of the butadiene and amine tanks mainly operated by ICI. However, by the early 1980s modern, German-owned bogie tanks had taken over these traffics, and the British-registered four-wheelers were largely withdrawn.

Anhydrous ammonia tanks, 40 t glw

All three batches of 40 t glw anhydrous ammonia tank wagons were of similar appearance, being vacuum-braked with a slightly smaller tank barrel than those fitted to petroleum wagons. Centrally-mounted side-ladders provided access to the top filling-hatch which was protected by a large metal plate, while buffer over-ride protec-

tion was fitted as standard at each end of the underframe.

The majority were operated by ICI from its plant at Haverton Hill, near Billingham, to various destinations including Heysham, Leith and Severn Beach, and carried the statutory livery of white tank with orange horizontal stripe. Solebars were painted orange with all lettering in black. A handful of wagons from the STS-owned batch were hired to Fisons Fertilizers for a while and could be identified by their green solebars, although otherwise their livery was identical. In 1984, the entire fleet was withdrawn and replaced by a varied number of air-braked bogie tank wagons.

Carbon dioxide tanks, 46 t glw

Carbon dioxide, mainly for use in the drinks industry, is also transported as a liquid under pressure, although there are none of the toxic hazards associated with

Another wagon built for continental traffic is this carbon dioxide tank, photographed at Ardwick in April 1986. Note the unusual end construction of the tank as well as the end platform and chaining-down lugs. Continental traffic in CO_2 had ceased by 1984 and this entire batch was leased to the Distillers Company. STS 53231 carried a white and orange livery with red tank lettering and black underframe.

the conveyance of chlorine, or the inflammable dangers present with LPG. In consequence, there is no need for elaborate tank protection, although the requirements of a reinforced barrel limit capacity to 28 t.

The first 19 wagons were built in Scotland by the Motherwell Bridge & Engine Company, the remainder, including a batch of 31 wagons intended for continental working, appearing from France during the 1970s. All are to the same basic design with a large tank and 15 ft wheelbase underframe, the earlier wagons being fitted with air brakes in 1982. By 1976, the entire fleet was on hire to the Distillers Company for operation within Britain and they have become a common sight in Speedlink services from Scotland and the North-east to destinations in Manchester, London and Birmingham.

Table 29: *Caustic soda, acid and solvent tanks, 46–51 t glw*

Type	Number series		TOPS code	Builder	Date	Owner/Operator
Caustic soda	BPCM	53601–53618	TTV	Central Wagon	1966	BP Chemicals, Murgatroyd
Caustic soda	BRT	57194–57243	TTF	Pressed Steel	1965	BRTE/ICI Mond
Caustic soda	BRT	57588–57637	TTB	Rootes Pressings	1966-7	BRTE/ICI Mond
Caustic soda	BRT	57697–57746	TTB	Metro Cammell	1966	BRTE/ICI Mond
Caustic soda	ICIM	70800–70819	TUA	Procor	1977	ICI Mond
Caustic soda	PR	58400–58405	TTB	Standard Wagon	1971	Procor/BP Chemicals
Caustic soda	PR	58501–58780	TTB	Standard Wagon	1968–72	Procor/various
Caustic soda	PR	70138–70149	TUA	Procor	1976	Procor/various
Caustic soda	TRL	51586–51548	TTB	Charles Roberts	1967	Tiger Rail/various
Caustic soda	TRL	70700–70727	TUA	Standard Wagon	1977	Tiger Rail/various
Hydrochloric acid	PR	58200–58211	TTB	Standard Wagon	1966	Procor/ICI Mond
Sodium hypochlorite	PR	58212–58220	TTB	Standard Wagon	1966	Procor/ICI Mond
Phosphoric acid	PR	58410–58425	TTB	Standard Wagon	1968	Procor/various
Phosphoric acid	PR	58901–58909	TTB	Standard Wagon	1968	Procor/various
Phosphoric acid	PR	70001–70022	TUB	Standard Wagon	1972	Procor/Albright & Wilson
Nitric acid	MODA	56950–56951	TTB	Powell Duffryn	1976	Ministry of Defence, Army
Nitric acid	TRL	51948–51953	TTA	Procor	1983–4	Tiger Rail/UKF Fertilizers
Sulphuric acid	BRT	57308–57322	TTF	Powell Duffryn	1966	BRTE/ISC Chemicals
Sulphuric acid	BRT	57845–57850	TTF/B	Powell Duffryn	1968	BRTE/ISC Chemicals
Sulphuric acid	TRL	51100–51116	TTA	Procor	1983	Procor/ISC Chemicals
Hydrocyanic acid	LS	54600–54609	TTB	Charles Roberts	1971	Lloyds & Scottish/ICI Mond

Type	Number series		TOPS code	Builder	Date	Owner/Operator
Hydrocyanic acid	PR	70162–70182	TUA	Procor	1980	Procor/ICI Mond
Hydrocyanic acid	TRL	51435–51449	TTV	Charles Roberts	1965	Tiger Rail/ICI Mond
Hydrocyanic acid	TRL	70734–70748	TUA	Procor	1980	Tiger Rail/ICI Mond
Acetic acid	ALG	49367–49390	TTB	L.H. Busch	1975	Algeco/BP Chemicals
Acetic acid	STS	53092–53106	TTB	Procor	1976	STS/BP Chemicals
Acetic acid	STS	53300–53366	TTA	Various	1966–72	STS/BP Chemicals
Acetic acid	23 70	7397 125–139	TIB	Rootes Pressings	1966–7	STS/BP Chemicals
General acids	23 70	7390 027–031	TIA	CFMF, France	1979	STS/various
Solvent	PR	58300–58313	TTB	Standard Wagon	1966–70	Procor/ICI Mond
Solvent	PR	58947–58955	TTB	Procor	1980	Procor/ICI Mond
Solvent	TRL	51954–51968	TTA	Procor	1985	Tiger Rail/Shell Chemicals
Sovent	23 70	7190 419–421	TIX	Charles Roberts	1964	Tiger Rail/various
Solvent	43 70	7499 300–301	TIB	Charles Roberts	1969	Tiger Rail/Shell Chemicals

Notes   Caustic soda tank wagons BRT 57194–57243 were modified with the fitting of Class A tank barrels in the late 1970s, and have subsequently been operated by both Carless Solvents and Petrofina.

Caustic soda tanks, 46–51 t glw

Most numerous of all chemical tank wagons are those built to carry the highly corrosive liquid caustic soda, which is widely used in various chemical processes. The two major British producers, ICI and BP Chemicals, each owned a small batch of caustic soda tanks, although the majority are leased from BRTE, Procor or Tiger Rail.

All the 46 tonners are of similar 'monobloc' construction, and are usually fitted with side-ladders and a small central catwalk around the top filler. The common 15 ft wheelbase underframe remained standard until 1976 when the first 51 t glw vehicles were introduced and it was lengthened to 16 ft, while various types of pedestal suspension were introduced, many

BP Chemicals, Murgatroyd Works, owned 19 46 t caustic soda tanks, unusually fitted with end-ladders and a short catwalk. When photographed at Hoo Junction in the late 1970s, BPCM 53614 had a light grey tank with a green and yellow 'BP' shield on a white ground; 'chemicals' was in light blue, with other lettering in white, and a black underframe (D. Larkin).

Above *BRT 57731, recorded at Runcorn in June 1985, illustrates the more common design of 46 t caustic soda tank with a central ladder. The tank livery is dark grey with white lettering, some on black patches. The 'BRT' symbol is in red, black and white; the solebars are orange, and the running gear black.*

Below *TRL 70701 is a 51 t caustic soda tank, originally leased to ICI Mond. However, by 1987, in common with this entire batch, it no longer operated from Runcorn, being used instead on a working from Ellesmere Port to Ulverston. The livery comprises a grey tank with white lettering and yellow 'Tiger' name. The ICI emblem has been painted out, although the orange solebars, a common feature on the ICI fleet, have been retained. The running gear is black. Ellesmere Port, May 1987.*

of the older vehicles subsequently being resprung for further use in main-line services.

Since 1975, all caustic soda tank wagons have been air-braked, the batch BRT 57194–57243 being withdrawn from service that year following a serious accident at Weaver Junction involving a partially-fitted train of such vehicles. During the 1970s, caustic soda tanks could be found in all the major industrial areas, in general BP Chemicals supplying destinations in the south of England from their works at Baglan Bay, South Wales, and ICI Mond the remainder of the country from Runcorn. However, in 1983 BP ceased to use rail for this commodity and many wagons previously on hire to them were either withdrawn or converted for other traffics, while ICI has also reduced the size of its hired fleet in recent years.

To provide additional capacity following the Weaver Junction accident, a number of wagons from the PR 582xx batch were fitted with tanks recovered from withdrawn, vacuum-braked caustic soda wagons. PR 58212 is one such vehicle, seen at Stoke in May 1987, after being fitted with parabolic springs to permit 60 mph running. The standard livery of grey tank with white lettering and orange solebar applied to the purpose-built caustic soda tanks operated by ICI Mond is also carried by PR 58212.

PR 58648 is another rebuilt tank wagon, being constructed in 1968 for caustic soda traffic with BP Chemicals. By 1984 it had been fitted with two filling points, new drainage channels and a modified ladder for further use with UKF Fertilisers carrying phosphoric acid. Livery comprises white for the top three-quarters of the tank barrel and brown for the remainder, the wing plates and the underframe. 'UKF' is brown, 'Fertilisers' light green and other lettering either white or yellow on black patches while the drainage channels are picked out in black. Ince, November 1984.

Acid and solvent tanks, 40–51 t glw

In addition to caustic soda, ICI Mond also produces a range of acids and solvents at its Runcorn and Fleetwood plants, for which a small number of 46 t glw tank wagons were constructed by Standard Wagon between 1966 and 1970. All are of similar design with air-braked, 15 ft wheelbase underframes, although detail differences exist with regard to the tank fittings dependent on which chemicals are handled.

Standard Wagon also built two small batches of very similar 46 t glw tanks for carrying phosphoric acid. Originally operated by Fisons Fertilizers, all 25 vehicles were transferred to UKF Fertilizers' use in 1981, when they were fitted with double-fillers, buffer over-ride plates, and repainted in an attractive brown and white livery. They normally run in block-train formations

In 1966, Standard Wagon built a number of 46 t tank wagons for acid and solvents traffic with ICI Mond. PR 58219, photographed stored out of use at Fleetwood in September 1987, was originally allocated to sodium hypochlorite traffic, being modified in the early 1970s with rubber spillage sheets fixed to the side of the tank to allow it to carry the highly corrosive hydrochloric acid. The livery is a blue-grey tank with white lettering, orange solebars and black running gear.

PR 58300 is a similar 46 t tank wagon, built by Standard Wagon for ICI Mond solvent traffic. Detail differences with PR 58219 include the position of the ladder and tank fittings, but the underframe is standard apart from the fitting of parabolic suspension. Livery is as for PR 58219 with the addition of the 'Trichloroethylene' branding in black and white. Runcorn, June 1986.

PR 58947, one of a small batch of tank wagons rebuilt from redundant hydrocyanic acid tanks in 1980 for solvents traffic, was recorded at Runcorn in May 1986. This particular vehicle carries methyl chloroform, known as 'Genklene LV', and is in the standard grey livery with orange solebars and black running gear.

between the Albright & Wilson plant at Corkickle, near Whitehaven, and Ince.

Also built by Standard Wagon for phosphoric acid were 22 51 t glw tank wagons fitted with English Steel pedestal suspension and a 16 ft wheelbase underframe. Livery comprises a green tank with black lettering and underframe, and these vehicles are used as a block-train service between Corkickle and Barton-on-Humber.

Only eight 46 t glw nitric acid tank wagons are listed in Table 29, two owned by the Ministry of Defence which work from Bishopton, and six leased by Tiger Rail to UKF Fertilizers, for operation between Ince and the BNFL works at

Springfield, while the few 46 t glw sulphuric acid tank wagons have all operated to the account of ISC Chemicals, from their smelting plant at Avonmouth. The two batches owned by BRTE were purpose-built, but none survived in use after 1983, the demand for an air-braked fleet seeing their replacement by a batch of 16 former chlorine tanks, modified by Procor and re-painted in a dark blue livery.

Although not a liquefied gas, hydro-cyanic acid, because of its highly poisonous nature, is conveyed in tank wagons of a similar type to those used for liquefiable gases. The original fleet comprised 15 vacuum-braked 46 t glw vehicles owned by Tiger Rail, to which were added a further

TRL 70737, a 51 t hydrocyanic acid tank wagon, recorded at Stoke in March 1987. Note the provision of over-ride protection plates along the top of the solebars as well as above the headstocks. The livery comprises a white tank with orange waist-level stripe, solebars and ends. The number panel is white and black while both the 'ICI' and 'TRL' symbols and all other lettering are in black on yellow patches (T. Mann).

10 air-braked wagons in 1971. However, the Lloyds and Scottish tanks lasted less than ten years in service before being replaced by a larger fleet of 51 t glw wagons owned by Procor and Tiger Rail. This traffic operates between Grangemouth and Billingham in block-train formations, usually comprising four or five tank wagons, with a brake-van and two of the special barrier wagons, detailed in Chapter 9, at each end.

The acetic acid tank wagons listed in Table 29 are all operated by BP Chemicals from its plant at Saltend, near Hull. The largest batch, STS 53300–53366, was built by Metro Cammell and IMC, Hartlepool,

and all have stainless steel clad tanks and 15 ft wheelbase, air-braked underframes. Two further batches, one owned by Algeco, were added in the mid 1970s to replace the similar 40 t glw ferry-fitted tanks which had previously been in use. In addition to acetic acid, these tanks are also used to carry acetone, ethanol, and isopropanol from the BP Chemicals plant at Baglan Bay.

The majority of the Tiger Rail solvent tanks are operated by Shell Chemicals and carry acetone and toluene from its refinery at Stanlow to destinations in Scotland and the South-west. The largest of the three batches was built in 1985 using tanks and underframes recovered from a selection of

STS 53097, an acetic acid tank operated by BP Chemicals, photographed at Tees Yard in September 1987. The livery comprises a stainless steel tank with black lettering and a red and white 'STS' symbol. Solebars are red and running gear black.

Also noted in Tees Yard in September 1987 was ALG 49386, another acetic acid tank wagon leased to BP Chemicals. Note the use of English Steel Pedestal suspension in contrast to the Gloucester Pedestal fitted to STS 53097. Livery is identical to that carried by the STS tanks apart from the addition of the 'Algeco' name in black and yellow.

Amongst the small batch of solvent tanks introduced by Tiger Rail in 1985 are three vehicles rebuilt with tank barrels recovered from old ferry tanks, including TRL 51963, noted at Ellesmere Port in October 1987. The livery is a light grey tank with the 'Tiger' symbol in black and yellow and other lettering black on a yellow patch, and white on black patches. The solebars are red and the running gear black.

redundant vehicles, amongst them the three ferry-fitted tanks built by Charles Roberts in 1964 which had previously been

in use with Distillers Chemicals. All solvent tanks currently operated by Shell and BP carry the statutory Class A livery.

Table 30: *Other tanks, 40–51 t glw*

Type	Number series		TOPS code	Builder	Date	Owner/Operator
Ammonium nitrate	FF	55408–55412	TTF	Charles Roberts	1965	Fisons Fertilizers
Glycol	TRL	51177–51232(r)	TTV	Charles Roberts	1962–3	Tiger Rail/ICI Organics
Glycol	TRL	51824–51829	TTF	Charles Roberts	1966	Tiger Rail/ICI Organics
Cyclohexane	TRL	51895–51947	TTB	Charles Roberts	1969–71	Tiger Rail/ICI Organics
Cyclohexane	TRL	55520–55525	TTA	Standard Wagon	1978	Tiger Rail/ICI Organics
Methanol	BRT	57000–57040	TTV	Powell Duffryn	1962	BRTE/various
Methanol	BRT	57295–57305	TTF	Powell Duffryn	1965	BRTE/ICI Agricultural
Methanol	BRT	57345–57349	TTF	Powell Duffryn	1967	BRTE/ICI Agricultural
Methanol	ICIA	54351–54380	TTB	Standard Wagon	1970	ICI Agricultural Division
Acetaldehyde	23 70 7190 346–352		TIX	Charles Roberts	1964	Tiger Rail/BP Chemicals
Amines	23 70 7190 399–408		TIX	Charles Roberts	1964	Tiger Rail/ICI Agricultural Division
Amines	23 70 7286 409–418		TIX	Charles Roberts	1964	Tiger Rail/ICI Agricultural Division
General purpose	23 70 7490 050–051		TIX	Charles Roberts	1966	Hauser/various
General purpose	23 70 7390 635–671(r)		TIB	Various	1964–5	Whyte Chemicals
Ethylene dibromide	AO	55319–55338	TTA	Various	1966–74	Associated Octel
Phosphorous	AW	53501–53524(r)	TTV	M.W. Grazebrook	1953	Albright & Wilson
Clay Slurry	STS	53111–53130	TTA	Various	1966–71	STS/various
Clay Slurry	TRL	51408–51409	TTV	Charles Roberts	1965	Tiger Rail/Inveresk Paper
Water	CC	55526–55530	TTA	Standard Wagon	1966–7	Chipmans Chemicals
Water	FA	56960–56965	TTV/F	Various	1964–5	Fisons Agrochemicals
Milk	MMB	42866–42870	TTF	W.H. Davis	1981	Milk Marketing Board

Other chemical tanks, 40–46 t glw

The remaining chemical tank wagons are all listed in Table 30. These include five 40 t glw anchor-mounted vehicles owned by Fisons Fertilizers which were used to carry ammonium nitrate until 1983, and a

batch of 20 six-wheel anchor-mounted phosphorous tanks built in 1953 for Albright & Wilson. Axle-load restrictions on Portishead quay, where the phosphorus was loaded, necessitated the use of three axles, these unique 40 t glw wagons being used to supply factories in

Above *Albright & Wilson's phosphorus tank No 5, seen at Crewe in October 1969. This six-wheel tank, which eventually became AW 53505, was painted silver with black ladders, pipework and catwalk; the under-frame was black with white lettering. Unfortunately, the livery of the large nameboard carried on the side of the tank is not known (D. Rowland).*

Below *AO 55335 is a 46 t ex-ferry tank used to carry ethylene dibromide. Because of the density of the load, only a small tank is needed. The livery comprises a mid-grey tank with blue and white 'Octel' plate and black lettering. The underframe is black with white lettering. Ellesmere Port, May 1987.*

Kirkby, Widnes and Oldbury until withdrawal in 1976.

Other chemical tanks included two small batches of 40 t glw 'monobloc'-type wagons hired to ICI Organics for glycol traffic, as well as a larger number of air-braked vehicles designed to carry cyclohexane, an important intermediate in the manufacture of nylon. However, none of these specialist wagons remained in use by 1985, while of the various Class A tank wagons dedicated to methanol traffic, only the air-braked fleet owned by ICI remained in use after 1984.

The seven acetaldehyde tanks owned by Tiger Rail were also withdrawn in 1985. They were originally operated by BP Chemicals between Grangemouth and the Continent, and apart from the addition of ferry fittings were basically standard Class A wagons, as are the two 40 t glw tanks owned by P. Hauser and the five 40 t glw tanks owned by Whyte Chemicals.

Finally in this category are the 20 ethylene dibromide tank wagons owned by Associated Octel. All were built as ferry wagons and carried 12-digit numbers until their reallocation to the Amlwch–Ellesmere Port service in 1980, although following accident damage a number were rebuilt by Standard Wagon in 1981 with new underframes and Gloucester pedestal suspension. Livery comprises a grey tank with black lettering and underframe.

Clay slurry, water, and milk tanks, 46 t glw

The advantages to certain customers of transporting china clay as a slurry was realized in the mid 1960s, and in 1966 Storage & Transport Systems introduced 18 purpose-built tanks, intended to operate as a block-train between Cornwall and the Bowater paper mill in Kent. A further two

---

CC 55528 began life in 1966 as VIP Petroleum number 018. Under TOPS it became VIP 55218 before being sold to Procor for use in methanol traffic as PR 55218. In 1986, it was resold to Chipmans Chemicals, renumbered CC 55528, and rebuilt as a TTA. Despite the legend on the side, this vehicle has been used to carry de-icing fluid from Haltwhistle in addition to its duties in the Chipmans Weedkilling Train. The livery is overall black with white lettering. Horsham, September 1987 (A. Prime).

FA 56960 was purchased from BP Oil in 1984 for use with the Fisons Weedkilling Trains. When seen at Castleton in August 1987, it had been recently repainted, the tank in emerald green with white stripe and lettering, the solebars red and the running gear black.

vehicles were added in 1971, built by IMC, Hartlepool, to the same design as the previous batch from Rootes Pressings. In appearance, these slurry tanks resemble caustic soda wagons although they have always been painted in a distinctive blue livery, originally enhanced by the Bowater symbol, and later by that of English China Clays.

The two slurry tanks leased to Inveresk Paper also operate from Cornwall, but to destinations in Scotland. They have larger diameter tank barrels than the STS wagons and were only fitted with air brakes in 1981. Livery is again a pale blue tank, in this case with extensive white lettering, and black underframe.

Both Chipmans Chemicals and Fisons Agrochemicals have purchased a few

redundant 46 t glw Class A tank wagons for use as water carriers. The Chipmans vehicles, which also carry the occasional load of de-icing fluid from Haltwhistle, are all former VIP tanks, while Fisons have acquired their tanks from BP Oil.

The five 46 t glw tanks owned by the Milk Marketing Board are also former Class A wagons, in this case previously owned by Texaco. They were modified by W.H. Davis in 1981 with the fitting of stainless steel cladding and a new discharge outlet in order to provide additional emergency capacity, and they are stored in company with the remainder of the Board's fleet at various strategic locations in the West Country. A similar livery to that found on the six-wheel milk tanks was also applied to these vehicles.

Chapter 12

Bogie Tank Wagons

Bogie tank wagons have become an increasingly important part of the private owner fleets since the introduction of the first 92 t glw prototype in 1966, and are now employed in a wide range of oil, chemical and other traffics.

Table 31: *Petroleum product tanks, bogie*

Type	Number series		TOPS code	Builder	Date	Owner/Operator
Class A	ESSO	78040	TCW	South Staffs Wagon	1966	Esso Petroleum
Class A	SUKO	87000	TDB	Metro Cammell	1966	Shell (UK) Oil
Class A	SUKO	80100–80121	TEA	Various	1967–8	Shell (UK) Oil
Class A	SUKO	80500–80542	TEB	Various	1967–8	Shell (UK) Oil
Class A	SUKO	87100–87359(r)	TEA	Various	1967–8	Shell (UK) Oil
Class A	SUKO	87500–87559	TEB	Various	1967–9	Shell (UK) Oil
Class A	BPO	80160–80168	TEA	Various	1967–8	BP Oil
Class A	BPO	80560–80578	TEB/A	Various	1967–8	BP Oil
Class A	BPO	87160–87263(r)	TEA	Various	1967–8	BP Oil
Class A	BPO	87460–87894(r)	TEB/A	Various	1967–9	BP Oil
Class A	STS	86000	TDB	Fauvet Girel	1968	STS/Esso Chemicals
Class A	BRT	84000–84041	TEB	R.Y. Pickering	1967	BRTE/various
Class A	BRT	84049–84089	TEB	Various	1967–8	BRTE/various
Class A	BRT	84110–84127	TEA	Metro Cammell	1969	BRTE/Murco
Class A	BRT	84146–84173	TEB	Charles Roberts	1969	BRTE/Mobil
Class A	BRT	84205	TEA	Powell Duffryn	1971	BRTE/various
Class A	BRT	84290–84300	TEA	Standard Wagon	1973	BRTE/various
Class A	BRT	84311–84321	TEA	Standard Wagon	1973	BRTE/various
Class A	PR	82612–82631	TEB	Charles Roberts	1970	Procor/various
Class A	PR	82642–82679	TEA	Metro Cammell	1969	Procor/various
Class A	PR	82709–82719	TEB	Standard Wagon	1968	Procor/Mobil
Class A	PR	82730–82773	TEA	Procor	1978–86	Procor/various
Class A	MURC	83500–83517	TEA	Procor	1981	Murco Petroleum
Class A	ALG	82000–82026	TEB	Various	1968–71	Algeco/various
Class A	CLMI	84800	TEB	Metro Cammell	1968	CLMI/Petrofina
Class A	GULF	84900–84909	TEB	R.Y. Pickering	1967–8	Gulf Oil
Class A	LS	85000–85004	TEB	Metro Cammell	1968	Lloyds & Scottish/Esso
Class A	LS	85021–85026	TEA	Charles Roberts	1970	Lloyds & Scottish/Gulf
Class A	AMOC	82311–82316	TEB	Standard Wagon	1969	Amoco
Class A	STL	85701–85743(r)	TEA	CFPM, France	1968–70	E.G. Steele/various
Class A	FINA	85500–85527	TEB	Various	1969–81	Petrofina

TOPS

Type	Number series	code	Builder	Date	Owner/Operator
Class A	PP	85200–85219	TEA	Charles Roberts	1970	Phillips Petroleum
Class A	RLS	82200–82213	TEA	Standard Wagon	1980	Railease/Total Oil
Class A	TOTL	85900–85974	TEA	Various	1978–87	Total Oil
Class A	TRL	86848–86881(r)	TEB	Charles Roberts	1968	Tiger Rail/Total Oil
Class A	TRL	86894	TEB	Charles Roberts	1968	Tiger Rail/various
Class A	33 70 7899 041–060		TIA	Arbel Fauvet, France	1987	Tiphook Rail/various
Class B	SUKO	83000–83759(r)	TEA/B	Various	1967–72	Shell (UK) Oil
Class B	BPO	83060–83399(r)	TEA	Various	1968–72	BP Oil
Class B	BPO	83560–83799(r)	TEA/B	Various	1967–8	BP Oil
Class B	BRT	84042–84180(r)	TEB	Various	1967–70	BRTE/various
Class B	BRT	84193–84202	TEB	Charles Roberts	1971	BRTE/Mobil
Class B	BRT	84241–84310(r)	TEA/B	Standard Wagon	1970	BRTE/Gulf Oil
Class B	PR	82600–82611	TEB	Standard Wagon	1969	Procor/Chevron Oil
Class B	PR	82632–82708(r)	TEB	Various	1969–72	Procor/various
Class B	PR	82720–82729	TEA	Standard Wagon	1972	Procor/Esso
Class B	GULF	84910–84926	TEB	R.Y. Pickering	1967–8	Gulf Oil
Class B	LS	85005–85020	TEB	Charles Roberts	1970	Lloyds & Scottish/Amoco
Class B	LS	85027–85048	TEA	Metro Cammell	1969–70	Lloyds & Scottish/Gulf Oil
Class B	AMOC	82301–82310	TEB	Powell Duffryn	1968	Amoco
Class B	AMOC	82317–82328	TDA	CFMF, France	1973–4	Amoco
Class B	AMOC	78900–78929	TCA	CFMF, France	1975–7	Amoco
Class B	STL	85731–85740	TDA	CFPM, France	1972	E.G. Steele/Amoco
Class B	FINA	85600–85652(r)	TEB/A	Various	1969–83	Petrofina
Class B	RLS	82214–82227	TEA	Standard Wagon	1981	Railease/Total Oil
Class B	TRL	86861–86876	TEB	Charles Roberts	1968	Tiger Rail/Total Oil
Class B	TRL	86882–86891	TEB	Charles Roberts	1968	Tiger Rail/Total Oil

Notes Shell (UK) Oil tank wagons occupy the number range 00–59.
BP Oil tank wagons occupy the number range 60–99.
In 1985, Phillips Petroleum sold their bogie tank wagons, PP 85200–85219, to T.P. Dibden and they were subsequently re-prefixed TPD.
In 1986, Lloyds & Scottish disposed of their entire bogie tank fleet, each batch being sold to its respective hirer and re-prefixed accordingly.
RLS 82214–82227 originally carried Class A livery but were also lagged to facilitate the handling of Class B products.

Esso Petroleum and Shell Mex & BP petroleum tanks, bogie

Esso, so often at the forefront of wagon innovation, introduced the first chassis-less tank wagon in 1966 for Class A products; it was a revolutionary 82 t glw design using aluminium for the tank, which had an elliptical cross-section. Welded construction was used for the barrel which had one internal stiffening ring at mid-length, with a double-sided ladder at one end to provide access to the full-length catwalk and loading hatches.

Built by Gloucester-Saro, and assembled by South Staffs Wagon at Tipton with Gloucester secondary coil suspension bogies, ESSO 78040, as the vehicle eventually became, underwent extensive trials, but the high cost of aluminium told against it and no more appeared. Air brakes were fitted in 1982 and the tank was transferred to Scotland to work on local services from the Bowling oil terminal.

At the same time as the chassis-less tank was being developed, Metro-Cammell was building a 92 t glw prototype Class A tank for Shell Mex & BP, to a design which proved to be the forerunner for most future bogie tank construction. Given the strength of the tank barrel, continuous solebars were not needed, the barrel being secured only to two short sections of solebar situated over the bogies. The solebars were then angled downwards and inwards to join two steel members running along the underside of the tank which carried the brake gear and discharge pipes. Fitting of air-operated clasp brakes and English Steel primary coil suspension bogies allowed a 60 mph maximum speed.

At 54 ft 10 in long, this tank was designed to be twice the length of the then current two-axle tanks in order that filling-hatches and discharge outlets would still be compatible with existing installations. Access ladders to the full-length catwalk were fitted at diagonally opposite corners, while the statutory Class A livery of light grey was enhanced by two horizontal bands in white and yellow at waist level along each side of the tank. Separate Shell and BP badges in red and yellow, and yellow, green, white and red respectively, were also painted on the side of the barrel, while red solebars, black bogies and underframe fittings with white lettering completed the colourful scheme.

After the successful trials of the prototype, later numbered SUKO 87000, Shell Mex & BP began to purchase a considerable fleet of similar vehicles, all to the same basic design though uprated to 102 t glw to take full advantage of the increase in permitted axle-loads on certain routes to 25½ t. Metro Cammell, R.Y. Pickering and Powell Duffryn were all heavily involved in this construction programme, and by 1969 Shell Mex & BP had over 1,000 bogie tank wagons in service. All were allocated SMBP TOPS numbers in 1974 but few, if any, actually carried them before Shell and British Petroleum decided to abandon their joint distribution operation.

BPO 80566, a 102 t bogie tank wagon built to the non-continuous solebar design introduced by Metro Cammel in 1966. This particular vehicle, built by R.Y. Pickering in 1967, is fitted with 'Epikote lining' — an internal coating designed to protect against rust and scale especially for the carriage of aviation fuels — and carries the statutory Class A livery with the 'BP' shield in green and yellow. Ellesmere Port, May 1987.

SUKO 83655, a 102 t Class B lagged and coiled bogie tank, seen at Stoke in April 1987. Note the conical end, indicative of a lagged tank, and the heating pipe. The livery is black with white lettering.

The separate operation of the rail tanks was not obvious as neither Shell nor BP wagons carried company emblems after 1976, though ownership could be determined from the TOPS plate, new TOPS numbers being carried with either the SUKO or BPO prefix. Furthermore, both companies still use the same number coding system; 83xxx for all Class B bogie tanks, and 87xxx for all Class As other than those with epikote lining which carry an 80xxx number.

Both the Shell and British Petroleum bogie tank wagons are a common sight, the Shell vehicles operating from their refineries at Stanlow, near Ellesmere Port, and at Thameshaven, near Coryton; the BP tanks, as well as working out of Grangemouth and Grain, also carry crude oil from onshore wells situated in Lincolnshire and the south of England. Crude oil is treated as a Class A product, and in order to accommodate a large increase in this traffic since 1978, BP have converted a large number of their Class B bogie tanks into

Class A wagons by the removal of heating coils and lagging, repainting and renumbering.

Other petroleum tanks, bogie

The new bogie tank wagons opened the way for trainloads of 2,000 t and more, and following their successful introduction by Shell Mex & BP they were rapidly ordered by most of the other major oil companies. Construction, involving all the major wagon builders, continued steadily until 1974 when the oil crisis hit demand, particularly for the heavier Class B products such as heating oil.

The basic Metro Cammell design was widely adopted, though usually uprated to 102 t glw, particular exceptions including BRT 84205, another aluminium frameless Class A prototype developed for Esso, and PR 82730–82747, a further design of chassis-less tank introduced by Procor in 1978. These tanks have a barrel that incorporates a sunken central section of oblate

When recorded at Castleton in November 1987, BRTE Class A tank BRT 84027 was returning to the Phillips refinery at Port Clarence. Originally this batch were operated by Esso and traces of the initial livery, which featured a broad red rectangle and the Esso oval symbol along the side of the tank, can still be discerned beneath the dirt.

form, so as to increase capacity, and carry Class A liquids from the Phillips refinery at Port Clarence.

The only Class B tanks of less than 102 t glw listed in Table 31 are three French-built batches, all either owned or operated by Amoco. All have the same chassis-less design with very short stub-frames and are only 54 ft 2 in long with French Y25C bogies. STL 85731–85740 and AMOC 82317–82328 are rated at 92 t glw rather than the 82 t of AMOC 78900–78929, as

The single bogie tank wagon owned by CLMI, the Companie pour la Location de Material Industrial, CLMI 84800, a 102 t Class A vehicle, is leased to Petrofina and operates between Lindsey and Preston. The Class A livery is enhanced with the 'Fina' symbol in red and blue. Preston, September 1987.

In 1981, the first 16 Petrofina Class B tanks, FINA 85600–85615, were rebuilt as Class A vehicles by removing the lagging and heating coils. Renumbered and repainted in grey and red livery, they operate between Lindsey and Preston, and it was at the latter location that FINA 85518, the former FINA 85606, was recorded in September 1987.

they are lagged to enable them to carry the more viscous products, such as heavy fuel oil.

Use of the traditional English Steel bogie has given way in the 1980s to various other rigid-frame, primary coil suspension designs, including the Y25C, Gloucester GPS, and Schlieren, while one batch of Class B tanks operated by Chevron Oil, PR 82704–82708, was fitted with British Steel 'Axle-Motion' bogies.

Although the decline in demand for 'black' products since the mid 1970s has seen a number of Class B tanks either withdrawn or else converted for other traffics, petroleum movements are still of major significance to British Rail. Indeed, given the scale of the operation it would be im-

TOTL 85936 was built by Standard Wagon in 1987 using various parts recovered from earlier Total Oil Class A tanks which were being withdrawn. The livery is a grey tank with the 'Total' symbol in blue, red, orange and white; the full-length solebars are red and the Gloucester GPS bogies black. Heywood, December 1987.

possible to detail every working, although certain fleets are particularly common in some areas. In general, Total and Petrofina supply depots in the North-east, Yorkshire and the East Midlands from their joint refinery at Lindsey, near Immingham, while Gulf and Amoco, both with refineries at Milford Haven, supply depots in the South-west, the South, and the West Midlands. Mobil, the largest producer to operate an entirely leased fleet, supplies depots in East Anglia and the Home Counties from its refinery at Coryton.

All bogie Class A tanks carry the statutory livery of light grey tank with red solebars, although company policy differs as regards the use of identifying logos, while the Class B fleets are all painted an over-all black, only rarely lightened by anything other than white lettering.

Table 32: *Pressurized gas tanks, bogie*

Type	Number series	TOPS code	Builder	Date	Owner/Operator
LPG	ESSO 78000	TBB	Old Park Engineering	1967	Esso Petroleum
LPG	ESSO 78001–78027	TDB	Various	1968–9	Esso Petroleum
LPG	ESSO 78028–78039	TCB	Charles Roberts	1970	Esso Petroleum
LPG	ESSO 78041–78048	TCA	Procor	1978	Esso Petroleum
LPG	STS 78650–78653	TCB	Fauvet Girel	1968	STS/Esso Petroleum
LPG/ Propylene	PR 78533–78547	TCA	Norbrit Pickering	1974	Procor/various
Propylene	PR 78500–78511	TCB	Charles Roberts	1974	Procor/Shell Chemicals
Propylene	PR 78400–78402	TCB	Procor	1976	Procor/Shell Chemicals
LPG	SUKO 89500	TDB	Charles Roberts	1975	Shell (UK) Oil
LPG	SUKO 89501–89514	TDA	Procor	1980	Shell (UK) Oil
Chlorine	BPCM 77001–77039	TBV	Various	1959	BP Chemicals, Murgatroyd
Chlorine	BPCM 77040–77043	TBB	Standard Wagon	1969	BP Chemicals, Murgatroyd
Vinyl chloride	STS 86050–86062	TDB	Fauvet Girel	1972	STS/various
Anhydrous ammonia	BRT 78551–78562	TCA	Old Park Engineering	1969	BRTE/UKF Fertilizers
Anhydrous ammonia	BRT 84203–84204	TDA	Charles Roberts	1972	BRTE/UKF Fertilizers
Anhydrous ammonia	EURL 78600–78617	TCB	Fauvet Girel	1971	Eurolease/various
Anhydrous ammonia	STS 78654–78679	TCA	Fauvet Girel	1973–6	STS/various
Anhydrous ammonia	33 70 7892 000–023	TIB/A	Fauvet Girel	1968–9	STS/various
Anhydrous ammonia	33 70 7892 024–046	TIB	Waggon Union	1981	VTG/various
Anhydrous ammonia	33 70 7895 001–022	TIB	Waggon Union	1980	VTG/various
Anhydrous amines	83 70 7891 000–002	TIB	Fauvet Girel	1972	STS/ICI Agricultural

Liquid petroleum gas tanks, bogie

In 1967, Esso introduced the first bogie tank wagon designed to carry LPG. Fitted with Gloucester bogies centred at 40 ft 6 in, this 56 ft long, 71 t glw vehicle could carry 32 t. Originally vacuum-operated disc brakes were fitted, but following extensive trials the wagon was converted to air-braking before entering service in 1968. The tank was mounted on a narrow chassis situated inside the wheels, with a series of holes cut into the chassis cross-members to reduce weight, producing a most odd appearance. A single filler/unloading hatch was located towards the left-hand end of the tank, which was painted in the statutory livery of white with red bands towards each end. The Esso emblem was carried at the right-hand end of the side, with a large oblong red panel along the remainder; all lettering, bogies and fittings were black. Although a success, this prototype was rapidly overtaken by technical improvements and by 1974 had been stored out of use before eventually being donated to the Bristol Transport Museum for display at their Wapping Wharf site.

By the time Esso began to purchase a fleet of bogie LPG tanks, the axle limit had increased and most details of the production batch differed from the prototype. Thirty-nine tanks were ordered, ESSO 78001–78015 from Norbrit Pickering with Schlieren bogies, the rest from Charles Roberts with Y25C bogies. All were 92 t

One of three 87 t liquid gas tanks built by Procor in 1976 for propylene traffic, PR 78402, was photographed under repair at Stoke in May 1987. Note the non-continuous solebar design and French Y25C bogies. The livery comprises a white tank with an orange waist-level stripe, white lettering on red and black patches and a black underframe.

glw with a capacity of 46 t, and measured 55 ft 11 in in length with bogies centred at 42 ft 10 in. Two loading-hatches were provided on each side to speed up the operation, while the underframe construction was to the non-continuous solebar design outlined above. After five years in service, working out of Milford Haven and Fawley, ESSO 78028–78039, which had been volumetrically limited as they were built with lighter tensile steel, were down-rated to 86 t glw.

Dimensionally identical to the Esso LPG tanks, but rated at 87 t glw, were two further batches of liquid gas tanks built by Charles Roberts in 1974 and by Procor in 1976. Leased to Shell Chemicals, all 15 vehicles carry propylene between the BP

Chemicals plant at Baglan Bay, in South Wales, and the Shell factory near Partington, Cheshire. Also in 1974, Norbrit Pickering introduced a batch of chassis-less tank wagons for LPG. In this design, the tank barrel carries all the forces, the short stub-frames simply a means of transferring the weight of the load to the Schlieren bogies. Rated at 84 t glw, all were initially operated by Esso, but by 1978 a few were carrying propylene for Shell Chemicals. Procor also built a batch of eight chassis-less LPG tank wagons for Esso in 1978, rated at 81 t glw and fitted with Y25C bogies.

Shell also owns a small fleet of bogie LPG tanks which carry butane and propane from its refinery at Stanlow. The prototype, SUKO 89500, was introduced in 1975 by

SUKO 89500, the prototype 92 t bogie LPG tank introduced in 1975, is seen at Heywood in November 1987. Note the Gloucester GPS bogies, full–length solebars and end–ladder, the provision of which is unique to this batch of LPG tanks. The livery comprises a white tank with an orange waist-level stripe, a red and yellow 'Shell' symbol, and black lettering and underframe.

Shell Mex & BP and is 55 ft 3 in long with Gloucester GPS bogies centred at 41 ft 11 in. Fourteen similar wagons, but without the through vacuum pipe fitted to the prototype, were built by Procor in 1980.

Chlorine and vinyl chloride monomer tanks, bogie

BP Chemicals Murgatroyd Works, at Sandbach, owned a large and varied fleet of tank wagons, including a batch of 43 bogie vehicles for liquid chlorine. The first 39 were built in 1959 to a 64 t glw cradle-mounted design with a capacity of 37 t. Minor differences existed within this batch with regard to the shape of the end stanchions and cradle supports, but all were 30 ft 10 in long with Gloucester plateback bogies centred at 18 ft 2 in. Originally these tanks were lettered up 'Murgatroyd Works', but by 1969, when the change in legislation required a white tank with orange waist-level stripe, they carried the full 'BP Chemicals' lettering and badge in green, yellow and light blue.

In 1969, a further four liquid chlorine bogie tanks were built for BP Chemicals by Standard Wagon. Although to the same overall dimensions as the earlier vehicles, these four wagons were rated at 71 t glw and could carry 40 t, this increase having been achieved by the adoption of a 'monobloc' design. Gloucester cast steel bogies centred at only 17 ft 1 in were fitted, as were air brakes, although a vacuum through pipe was also necessary to allow running in company with the earlier batch to destinations at Baglan Bay, Fawley, Kings Lynn, Newport and Spondon. The last examples of this fleet were withdrawn from main-line use in 1984.

BP Chemicals also operated a fleet of STS-owned vinyl chloride monomer tanks built in 1972. At 50 ft 11 in long, these 92 t glw tanks present a substantial appearance with very deep, full-length solebars and Y25C bogies centred at 39 ft. The single filler-hatch is sited on the end of the tank with access from a small end platform. The original livery comprised a white tank with orange stripe, black numbers and white lettering on red panels. The BP 'shield' was green and yellow, with 'BP Chemicals' in light blue lettering and 'STS' initials in red. Solebars and bogies were black with white lettering.

In 1986, three of this batch had been given 12-digit numbers and were on hire to ICI to carry anhydrous amines to the Continent, but by 1987 all 13 tanks had reverted to vinyl chloride monomer traffic, though now operated by ICI. They run from the ICI plant at Thornton, near Fleetwood, to the BP Chemicals plant at Barry, where the monomer is transmuted into heavy-duty plastics.

Anhydrous ammonia tanks, bogie

Seven batches of bogie tank wagons have been introduced to carry liquid anhydrous ammonia, a highly toxic gas used in fertilizer manufacture. Twelve $82\frac{3}{4}$ t glw tanks with a payload of 46 t were built for BRTE in 1969 for hire to Shellstar, and were fitted with end brake platforms and chaining-down lugs for continental working. All had been withdrawn from use in Britain by 1982. BRTE also owns two 92 t glw ammonia tanks, built in 1972 with full-length solebars. They have Y25C bogies in place of the English Steel type fitted to the previous batch, and are without any ferry fittings, being leased to UKF Fertilizers to operate between Ince and Barton-on-Humber.

Also initially leased to UKF Fertilizers were the first 18 anhydrous ammonia tanks

STS 78678, an 88 t bogie anhydrous ammonia tank originally operated by Fisons Fertilisers. By the date of this photograph, taken at Immingham C & W in November 1987, this entire batch had been transferred to ICI and relettered accordingly. The tank livery is white with an orange waist-level stripe and black lettering, while the deep, angled solebars are green with white lettering; the bogies and underframe fittings are black.

from Fauvet Girel. Owned by Eurolease, a subsidiary of STS, they are very similar to the later batch introduced two years later for hire to Fisons Fertilisers. The main difference is the distinctive angled solebars fitted to the later batch, which also have Gloucester GPS bogies rather than Y25Cs, and at 88 t glw they are some 2 t heavier than the Eurolease vehicles. All are 57 ft 11 in long and can carry 53 t.

The three remaining batches of anhydrous ammonia tanks are all fully ferry-fitted and carry 12-digit numbers, although their use is largely confined to Britain. The STS vehicles are similar to the Eurolease tanks apart from the addition of an end platform, and were also initially operated by UKF Fertilisers. The VTG tanks are slightly larger and carry 50 t.

They are built to a non-continuous solebar design, one batch having a sun-shield fitted along the top of the tank. In 1984, the entire STS, VTG and Eurolease fleets were transferred to ICI and now operate from its Haverton Hill plant, near Billingham.

Latex and edible oil tanks, bogie

The dozen unfitted latex tanks owned by the Liverpool-based transport company, Henry Diaper, were built in 1941 to the standard design of the period with cradle-mounts, large end stanchions and centrally-located side-ladders. They were only 30 ft 9 in long with secondary coil suspension bogies centred at 17 ft 11 in and carried only 26 t. Although allocated TOPS numbers, it is unclear if this batch ever operated with

Table 33: *Other tanks, bogie*

Type	Number series		TOPS code	Builder	Date	Owner/Operator
Latex	HD	76013–76024	TAO	R.Y. Pickering	1941	Henry Diaper
Edible oil	VDBJ	82500–82523	TEA	C.C. Crumps	1986	Van Den Bergh & Jurgens
Nitric acid	BRT	84183–84192	TEA	Charles Roberts	1971	BRTE/various
Sulphuric acid	STL	85703–85710	TEA	Various	1970–76	E.G. Steele/Hays Chemicals
Cryogenic	BOC	84601–84640(r)	TEA	Charles Roberts	1969–70	British Oxygen Company
Clay slurry	TRL	78800–78804	TCA	CFMF, France	1975	Tiger Rail/various
Clay slurry	TRL	86895–86906	TDA	C.C. Crumps	1987	Tiger Rail/ECC
Clay slurry		33 70 7895 150–165	TIA	Various	1984–5	VTG/ECC
Clay slurry		83 70 7895 200–204	TIA	Ateliers, France	1987	STS/ECC
Sodium		33 70 7996 001–003	TIA	Standard Wagon	1985	Associated Octel
General purpose		33 70 7899 001–040	TIA	Arbel Fauvet, France	1987	Tiphook Rail/various

them, although the company continued to use rail until 1980.

The Van Den Bergh & Jurgens tanks carry imported edible oil, used in the manufacture of margarine and cooking oils, from Purfleet to Bromborough on the Wirral. All are converted Shell Class B tanks from the series SUKO 831xx, and have new pattern stainless steel heating coils and stainless steel cladding.

Van Den Bergh & Jurgens edible oil tank, VDBJ 82502, illustrated at the Connah's Quay works of C.C. Crump in March 1986 immediately prior to release into service. Converted from Shell Class B tank SUKO 83125, this 102 t vehicle has an unpainted stainless steel tank with black lettering and a black and white number panel. The underframe, ladders and catwalk are black with white lettering (T. Mann).

Acid tanks, bogie

The BRTE 102 t glw bogie acid tanks are only 39 ft 11 in long, with Schlieren bogies centred at 26 ft 2 in. They have stainless steel clad, rubber-lined tanks, with a ladder at each corner and an enclosed discharge outlet beneath the solebars. Carrying a 73 t load, the majority are operated by UKF Fertilizers and carry nitric acid from Ince to Sellafield, although at least three have been carrying sulphuric acid for Hays Chemicals, of St Helens, since 1986.

Also operated by Hays Chemicals are the eight sulphuric acid tanks owned by E.G. Steele, STL 85703–85710. All were built by CFMF to a frameless design, apart from STL 85709, constructed by Standard Wagon in 1976 with full-length solebars and a different-shaped ladder and catwalk. All eight tanks have English Steel bogies and are 44 ft 7 in long. When first introduced in 1970, they were based in St Helens, but since 1986 they have all been concentrated in the North-east and work out of Seal Sands.

BRT 84185, a 102 t nitric acid tank, photographed at Ince in November 1984. Note the provision of ladders at either end, full-length solebars and Schlieren bogies. The livery comprises an unpainted stainless steel clad tank and black underframe. 'UKF' is brown, 'Fertilisers' green on a white patch; the BRTE fleet number is black and the number panel white and black.

STL 85710, a 102 t sulphuric acid tank built by CFMF, France, in 1970 to its frameless design with English Steel bogies and single end-ladder. The Hays Chemicals livery comprises a royal blue tank with white lettering and black bogies. Tees Yard, September 1987.

The first of the British Oxygen Company's cryogenic bogie tank wagons, BOC 84601, recorded at Stoke in October 1986. Note the Gloucester cast steel bogies and the lack of ladders, all loading being through valves situated beneath the solebar. The livery comprises a white tank with a red waist-level stripe and red and white 'BOC' markings. The tank lettering is black, the underframe black with white lettering.

Cryogenic tanks, bogie

The British Oxygen Company owns a fleet of highly-specialized cryogenic tank wagons designed to carry liquified atmospheric gases. These impressive 102 t glw vehicles are 60 ft long with either Gloucester cast steel or GPS bogies centred at 40 ft, and have vacuum-insulated, stainless steel tank vessels suitable for carrying a payload of 56 t of oxygen (at a temperature of $-183°C$), or 48 t of nitrogen (at $-196°C$). Workings originate from Middlesbrough and the large BOC plant at Ditton, near Widnes, to depots throughout the country.

Clay slurry tanks, bogie

Traffic in china clay and chalk slurry, particulary for use in paper-making, has seen a considerable increase since the early 1980s, for which Tiger Rail has provided a number of bogie tanks made redundant from declining chemicals traffics. Amongst these are five 82 t glw wagons, TRL 78800–78804, previously leased to Leathers

Chemicals for sulphuric acid, which were modified in 1981 to carry china clay slurry from Cornwall to the Crosfields soap works at Warrington. In 1987, this traffic was taken over by redundant four-wheel caustic soda tanks, the bogie vehicles being transferred to Quidhampton and repainted in English China Clay livery.

In 1987, Tiger Rail also introduced a new batch of bogie slurry tanks for the Quidhampton traffic. All are 91 t glw vehicles, constructed by C.C. Crumps using underframes taken from redundant Class B bogie tanks, and tank vessels removed from stored four-wheel cyclohexane tanks.

English China Clay also operates a small number of ferry-fitted bogie tanks owned by VTG and STS. Built by Link Hoffman Busch and Waggon Union, the VTG wagons can carry 58 t and are normally used to supply customers in Scotland, while the five STS tanks, rebuilt using underframes and bogies recovered from redundant LPG and Class A vehicles, work from Quidhampton to Bowaters in Kent.

VTG bogie slurry tank, 33 70 7895 163–5, photographed passing Warrington in August 1987 whilst returning from Scotland to Quidhampton. Note the end platform, central ladders and underframe design as well as the bogies, a type of unknown design common on wagons owned by VTG. The overall livery is black with white lettering and blue and white 'ECC' symbol.

Other bogie tanks

In 1985, Associated Octel introduced three 80 t glw tank wagons specially built to carry sodium metal. Constructed by Standard Wagon, they are ferry-fitted and operate between Ellesmere Port and West Germany. Capacity is limited to 45 t, since to discharge the sodium, which is allowed to solidify before transportation, hot oil must be pumped into special heating tubes enclosed within the vessel. Livery comprises a stainless steel clad tank with black lettering and underframe.

Tiphook Rail also owns a batch of stainless steel insulated tanks, but these are 90 t glw general purpose vehicles suitable for carrying poisonous and corrosive liquids as well as inflammable chemicals.

General purpose 90 t bogie tank 33 70 7899 021–1 seen at Crewe in December 1987 when on display with the Tiphook Rail Freight Exhibition Train. The livery comprises an unpainted stainless steel clad tank with blue, orange and white 'Tiphook' logo. The wing plates are blue, solebars red, and the number plate and running gear black with white lettering.

Index

AFI 12, 14, 100, 114, 128
Atomic flask wagons 105
Axle-loads 7, 128, 131, 153

Barrier wagons 99, 101
Bogie bolster wagons
   104–106
Bogie steel wagons 105, 106
British Rail 7–9, 13, 25, 37,
   41, 50, 65, 71, 91, 106
Bulk powder wagons:
   Alumina 33, 35
   Barytes 33, 35
   Cemflo 25–27
   Metalair 28, 29
   Presflo 25–36
   Soda ash 32–35
   Tip-air 33, 35
   Tripolyphosphate 33, 34,
      81
   Twin-cone 30, 32, 82

Coaches:
   Escort 95, 98
   Weedkilling train 95–97
Containers:
   Coal 38, 82
   Curtain-sided 42–44
   Potash 38, 44
   Refuse 40–42, 82
   Salt 38
Couplings:
   AAR 63, 80, 102
   Instanter 63, 94
   International screw 94
   Rotary 89
Covered hopper wagons:
   Aggregate 13, 15

Alumina 13, 17–18
China clay 10, 13, 17–21,
   23
Clinker 20, 21
General purpose 10, 20,
   21, 24
Grain 13–15, 20, 23, 24
Iron ore 13, 16
Lime 13, 15–17
Petroleum coke 13, 17, 18
Sand 13, 19
Starch 20, 81
Tripolyphosphate 20
Urea 15, 22
Curtain-roof wagons 105,
   107

Dummy flask wagon 99, 104

Epikote lining 153, 154

Flat wagons:
   Conflat 37–46, 82
   Flat/Flatrol 41, 47–49, 83
   Prologie 41, 50
   Skip carrier 37, 40
   Tankflat 41, 47
   Warflat 41, 46, 47
   Warwell 41, 46
   Zinc block 37

Grainflow 23

Hot ingot wagons 105, 109

Linercrane 105, 108
Liner trains 37
LPG training tank 99, 103

Match wagons 99, 101, 102
Mineral wagons:
   China clay 71, 73
   Coal 71, 72
   Minerals 71–73
Ministry of Supply 118
Ministry of War Transport 7
Motor vehicle carrying
   wagons:
   Autic 65, 68, 69
   Carflat 65, 70
   Cartic 65–67
   Comtic 65, 69, 70
   'Procor 80' 65, 67, 68

Nuclear flask wagons 99,
   104, 105, 110

Open wagons:
   Aggregate 78, 80
   Building blocks 71, 76
   Concrete sections 78, 80
   Dropside, pallet 43, 78,
      79, 100
   Highfit 71, 73
   Scrap metal 71, 74–80
   Soda ash 71, 73
Open hopper wagons:
   Aggregate 51, 53–56, 58,
      59 61–64, 83, 84
   Ballast 59–61
   Demonstrator 51, 58, 59
   Gypsum 51, 57
   Iron ore 59, 61
   Limestone 51, 58–60
   Salt 51–53
   Sand 19

Polybulks 14, 15, 22–24

Ramp wagons 99, 104, 105, 108
RIV 22
Road railer 105
Rod coil wagon 99, 100
Runner wagons 99, 102, 103

'Section 8' grants 8, 75
Self-discharge hopper train 44, 51, 56
Southern Pacific Railway 9
Spacer wagons 99, 102
Speedlink 8–10
Steel coil wagons 105–107

Tank wagons:
  Acetaldehyde 147, 149
  Acetic acid 140, 145, 146
  Amines 137, 138, 147, 157, 160
  Ammonia 119, 120
  Ammonium nitrate 119–121, 147
  Anhydrous ammonia 134, 138, 157, 160, 161
  Anti-knock compound 119, 121
  Arcton 117, 118
  Bitumen 113, 116, 117, 127, 128, 131–133
  Bromine 86, 119, 122
  Butadiene 137, 138
  Carbon dioxide 134, 138, 139
  Caustic liquor/soda 88, 119, 120, 139–142
  Chlorine 87, 117, 118, 134, 136, 137, 157, 160

Cryogenic 162, 164
Cyclohexane 147, 149
De-icing fluid 119, 122
Edible oil 162
Ethyl chloride 134, 137, 138
Ethylene dibromide 119, 122, 147–149
General purpose 119, 122, 147, 148, 162, 165
Glycol 147, 149
Hexene 119, 122
Hydrochloric acid 118, 119, 139, 143
Hydrocyanic acid 139, 140, 144, 145
Latex 161, 162
Liquid Petroleum Gas 117, 134, 135, 157–160
Lubricants 113, 117, 128, 133, 134
Methanol 131, 147, 149
Milk 123–125, 147, 150
Molasses 123, 125, 131
Nitric acid 88, 118, 119, 139, 144, 162, 163
Petroleum 87, 113, 116, 126–131, 151–157, 162
Phosphoric acid 139, 142–144
Phosphorus 147–149
Propylene 157–159
Slurry 88, 147, 149, 150, 162, 164, 165
Sodium 162, 165
Solvents 119, 121, 122, 139, 140, 143–146
Sulphuric acid 118, 119, 139, 144, 162, 163
Tar 123

Vinyl chloride 157, 160
Water 123, 124, 147, 149, 150
Tank wagon design:
  Chassis-less 152, 154, 155, 159, 163
  Monobloc 7, 114, 128, 129
  Oblate barrel 154, 155
  Standard 35 t 7, 114, 115
Tippler wagons:
  Aggregate 90
  Demonstrator 76–78
  Ilmenite 76, 77
  In-line 78, 90
  Iron ore 76–78, 89
  Lime 76–78, 85, 90
  Salt 76
  Spoil 78, 90
TOPS 9
TOPS codes 9–12
Torpedo ladle wagons 105, 108, 109
Trailer Train 105, 110–112
Train Ferry services 22
Transfer wagons 44
Tube wagons 99, 100

UIC 11, 22, 46, 107, 110, 128, 131

Vans:
  Curtain-sided 85, 86, 91, 94, 95
  Ferry 95, 98
  Palvan 73, 86, 91–96, 100
  Railiner 91, 94
  Rail van 91, 94
  Ventilated 91, 92